CELEBRATING YOU WITH PR!

An Empowering PR Guide for female entrepreneurs to get confident, get visible, to get in the press

JO SWANN

CONTENTS

DEDICATION

For my little ones who I hope to inspire:
My gorgeous Jake who makes my heart swell everyday with his
kindness and fun-loving nature and my little monkey Oscar whose
cheeky character lights up a room.
I wonder what books you'll write one day...

Also...

Thank you to my amazing hubby who has learnt to live with my
laptop, I appreciate all you do - I promise!

Thank you to my awesome parents who've played many parts in
enabling to me to follow my heart and do work that I love.

A big up to my kick ass support network who drive me on. You've cheered and championed me, supported and guided me, picked me up, pushed me forward, and helped me hold on for the ride.

Lyndsey, Em, Mel, Dani, Zandra - THANK GOD for you my Menston power mums.

Abi, Sarah, Dani thank you from the bottom of my heart for always being Team Choc PR and seeing this book in me before I did!

Donna, Cheryl, Dawn, Caroline - big up to LA Breakfast Club and big love to Niyc for believing in me even when I don't.

Andrea, you know I wouldn't be here without your loving kick up the backside, and Jo M, my partner in crazy gold glittery fun, what would I do without you?

Finally a shoutout to all my amazing inspirational clients who have trusted me with your incredible stories, you make me proud everyday.

Thank you all x

I'm a lucky girl and I'm celebrating all of you and having you in my world x

FOREWORD

The Power of Celebration

Niyc Pidgeon

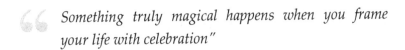

Something truly magical happens when you frame your life with celebration"

I remember the very first time I was featured in the media, with my first ever business back in 2012. I was featured in the local paper, and it felt like a big deal. Not only was it a great opportunity to get my business out there into the world, but it meant I was starting to get recognised as a young entrepreneur who was up to some good stuff.

And what's more, I was able to begin to acknowledge myself for the hard work and dedication I'd been putting in, and celebrate myself along the way too.

Every media feature I got, I shared with the world - and by "world" I mean my tiny corner of the internet, which at that time had around 1000 followers, mostly from my hometown, where I'd been showing up and sharing about positive psychology, the science of happiness and success, to anyone who would listen.

Sure, I was embarrassed, and nervous about what people might think, but I started small, and took it step by step, and leveraged every piece of media I would get. And you know what? Other people were watching... they started to listen... and they began to celebrate too.

Since then, and with Jo's help, I've reached more than 50 million people through the media, and have been featured in big names like Marie Claire, BBC, Money, mindbodygreen, Women's Health, Business Insider, Psychologies Magazine, goop, and was named as a Legendary Entrepreneur in Forbes.

You don't need to do it all at once - but you definitely do need to start. Sharing your celebrations for your mission, vision, and accomplishments along the way will bring you closer to yourself, closer to your community, and closer to your goals - and what's more, it's going to help you feel better more of the time too!

Throughout my career as an Award Winning Positive Psychologist, Best Selling Author, and Certified Coach, I've been reminded of the power of deeply connecting with others, and orienting ourselves towards what is good.

When you focus on what's good, you'll open up your thinking to more creative solutions, be able to reach your goals faster, feel more accomplished, more confident, and build better relationships too. And the main thing is... you truly deserve to celebrate YOU.

In this book you're going to discover your own excitement for sharing your truth, connecting with others through the power of your story, and being able to create more impact by leveraging media reach, than you ever could alone.

There's something extra special that starts to happen when you begin to make this shift and recognise that a celebration - and getting featured in the media - is a powerful tool to help you connect, get into momentum, grow within your relationships, and remind you of your purpose - and to help other people do that too.

I feel grateful to have had Jo by my side for my own PR and media, as well as her supporting our high level community of women entrepreneurs to get visible and get PR too.

Having worked closely together for a number of years now I've witnessed Jo's energy and expertise first hand, and know you're in the right place as you read these pages in Celebrate You. As well as motivating you to get out there and get seen, you're getting the tools and the steps to take action right away. This no-nonsense guide helps you get to know yourself, trust yourself, and show up and get seen like never before!

I invite you to take that next step and allow yourself to be guided by Jo to new levels of personal empowerment, certainty, and opportunity so you can grow your audience, have more impact, and get better business results too.

This book has the power to help you get your message out there to connect with the people who truly need your help. If you don't do it for you, do it for them - because people need to connect, relate, and feel inspired now more than ever before. You getting visible makes that possible.

This book will have you celebrating yourself a little louder, a little prouder, AND with Jo's support you'll be celebrating the bigger better results that come with it too - it's your time.

With Gratitude,

Niyc Pidgeon

Positive Psychologist MSc IPPA, Hay House Author "Now Is Your Chance", Certified High Performance Coach, Founder Of Unstoppable Success, & Positive Psychology Coach Academy Certification.

ABOUT THE AUTHOR

Jo Swann

Having grown up wanting to be a journalist Jo worked in radio, on news desks and as a magazine editor building her early career in the heart of the media, interviewing celebrities as well as sharing local people's stories but her passion these days lies in utilising the press to empower women in business - to help spread the messages of women on a mission, to help celebrate and showcase conversations that matter - and to change lives in the process.

Jo is the Founder of Chocolate PR, a creative PR agency she established over 17 years ago, after working in journalism, media, marketing and PR agencies. Over the years she has worked with companies including Whistles, NSPCC, learndirect, Yo! Sushi, Dale Carnegie, Skipton Building Society to name just a few, winning many awards along the way. However, she believes PR is for all of us, not just the big boys. Passionate about solopreneurs and female entrepreneurs particularly becoming empowered through coverage in the national press, she helps them gain credibility and third-party recognition.

Facing Imposter Syndrome head on she works with clients to create confidence in their message, helping them to craft their story in a way that makes them a *media magnet* as well as making them feel more comfortable about getting visible. Often referred to as a 'cheerleader' or 'champion' Jo is here to ensure your message doesn't go unheard and your story and contribution is celebrated.

Podcast - https://podfollow.com/pr-powerhouse

Facebook group -

https://www.facebook.com/groups/PRYouCanDoIt

Website - www.chocolatepr.co.uk

facebook.com/chocpr
instagram.com/jochocpr

PRAISE FOR CELEBRATING YOU

" With this book Jo has invited women to a party of empowerment. Each chapter enlightens you, strengthens you and celebrates you. It shows women how to come out of the shadows and step into the light. Jo's words inspire and ignite, showing the power of PR"

— LOTTIE LEEMING, BBC AND FREELANCE
BROADCAST JOURNALIST

" Jo gives you the confidence to own your story with passion and love. You can't find a better champion to help you Celebrate You!"

— NATALIE ANDERSON, ACTRESS

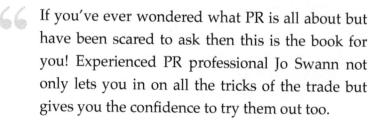

If you've ever wondered what PR is all about but have been scared to ask then this is the book for you! Experienced PR professional Jo Swann not only lets you in on all the tricks of the trade but gives you the confidence to try them out too.

Once she has got you engaged in the whole topic of PR and given you a self-esteem boost so you can overcome whatever is holding you back, Jo takes you through the all the different types of PR out there.

What's more, she gives you the ability to deal with the scary members of the press, tells you how to cope with rejection if your story is not picked up - and builds your self-belief so you are not put off.

I've no doubt that buying this book will give your business a boost!"

— LEBBY EYRES, NATIONAL JOURNALIST AND FORMER EDITOR IN CHIEF AT NEW! MAGAZINE

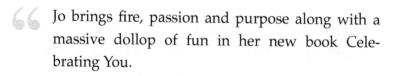

Jo brings fire, passion and purpose along with a massive dollop of fun in her new book Celebrating You.

It's like having Jo in the room with you - pouring Prosecco, giving you a sharp kick up the bum whilst simultaneously holding your hand and supporting you with love. This is Jo Swann in your pocket. Jo's voice, passion and expertise jumps off the page as she wills you to take advantage of your number one asset. YOU.

This book will rocket launch your brand and your business because it will show you that you really are the most important person at the party and how you can harness the power of PR to shine your message and purpose brightly so that everyone wants an invite! Don't miss the party!"

— LOUISA HERRIDGE, FOUNDER OF MAMAS
IGNITED

 So you're thinking of throwing a PR Party for yourself?! GOOD! You are in the safest of hands!

Jo Swann has been my go-to girl for PR from the minute I had the hare-brained notion of doing things a little differently in my industry to now, where, not only my business is nationally recognised, but I am too.

It's meant I've been able to help more people than I ever dared dream of and have more impact than I ever thought possible.

It is in no small part down to taking action on the advice and, let me be frank, solid bloody GOLD that Jo shares in this book. Read it, digest it, make a plan and FLY!

Stop waiting to be invited to the party, Cinders. Jo and this book are all the PR Party magic you need!

— DANI WALLACE, FOUNDER OF 'I AM THE QUEEN BEE' MOVEMENT AND THE FLY ANYWAY FOUNDATION

1

CHEERS!

S hout it loud!

Give me a: C: "C"

Give me an E: "E"

Give me an L: "L"

Give me an E: "E"

Give me a B: "B"

Give me a R: "R"

Give me an A: "A"

Give me a T: "T"

Give me a E: "E"

And what have you got...? Your mantra that's going to take you through these oncoming chapters, with passion and purpose that's what!

This is the chant we will be cheering at the end of this book when you truly step into *Celebrating You!*

This is a word that's going to mean a lot to you, as it does for me.

Welcome! Welcome to the party, welcome to your celebration, welcome to the journey of *Celebrating You.*

We're starting as we mean to go on because today is a day to celebrate. This is the start of something exciting for you, the start of your celebration of *you* and what *you* bring to the world. You quite possibly don't even know yet just how much you will be celebrating by the end of this book and the anticipation of that alone makes me want to do a big excited *'eeeekkkkk'* because your potential is so huge!

My mission is all around supporting female entrepreneurs to get more visible. To help you harness the power of PR to spread your message and amplify your impact through getting published in the press. I know this sounds scary and you might think I'm crazy at this point to suggest you could do such a thing but you're here right? You've bought this book which means you're up for the ride.

I love unravelling the mystery that often surrounds PR and helping business owners who previously thought PR was just for the big boys see it CAN be for them too, because the power of being in the media can supercharge businesses and ALL passion and purpose fuelled entrepreneurs deserve that! You most certainly do.

I particularly love working with women because the 'female entrepreneur' has a very special place in my heart. I know your struggles; I've walked your walk and I've felt the internal battles you feel.

In this book we won't just be talking about how to do PR but we'll be talking about how it feels to do PR and we'll be looking at some of the limits we place on ourselves in terms of why we might NOT do PR. I've lived this first-hand and have seen visibility fears come out through hundreds of our clients' journeys too, whether they've been in business two minutes, two years or twenty years.

So, welcome to *'Celebrating You!'*. This book, has taken two years to write and despite an award-winning career spanning twenty years working in journalism, PR and media and supporting brands such as Whistles, Yo Sushi, Dale Carnegie and NSPCC, as well as hundreds of start-ups too, it has taken me two years to get fully out there as the PR expert. I love pushing others into the limelight - *"stand there, pose like this, say this, say that"* - totally my forte, I'm cool with being bossy- but stepping into the spotlight myself is a whole new ball game, and one I haven't really wanted to play competitively until now.

The irony isn't lost on me believe me, and I have felt like a total idiot for behaving this way - a PR professional not using their voice. It's hardly leading from the front is it? But you see being centre stage isn't naturally my thing. Standing loud and proud to own my expertise has been a struggle.

I can thank the good old imposter syndrome voice in my head for that, spouting off all sorts of crap that has kept me 'playing safe' when I could have been out making much bigger waves. I guess I can also blame the bullying boss from agency days, who in retrospect, I realise, had squashed a bit of life and soul out of the feisty me when it came to standing up and being counted.

Well, it's time to say goodbye to all of that, because I feel differently today. Totally different. I can feel the excitement run through me that I'm finally emerging as the person I could have been two years ago when I originally signed up to write this book.

Connecting to this mission and my burning desire to see more women's incredible achievements celebrated in the press has led me here today. I am a purpose and passion fuelled entrepreneur just like you and I'm here to be your champion and cheerleader.

In the last twelve months I've launched a No.1 charting podcast, I have spoken on stages globally, I have attracted award nominations and incredible high-level partnerships.

You've joined me at the perfect moment, now I've stopped fucking about and procrastinating, but do you know what the bumps in the road have given me? A deeper empathy, an understanding of how you might be feeling as you start your journey on becoming more visible. If you're scared, I get it. If you're doubting yourself, I've felt it. If you're self-sabotaging your success, I've done it. But no more.

So, what's changed? How did this book get birthed? Why do I now feel like I have something worth writing? Why did I go from feeling terrified to excited about bringing this to life? Well, my lightbulb moment came when I decided this was to be my year of celebration.... a year celebrating my incredible clients, my awesome team, my gorgeous family - and myself. This is to be my year of leaning into this feeling of gratitude of the amazing people I have around me and the incredible energy I get from them. I also decided it was to be a year where I really celebrated and showcased my own skills as I KNOW how impactful they have been for those who've tapped into them- literally life changing in many cases.

My clients inspire me daily and you'll meet some of them within these pages. I decided I owed it to them to do this, as well as to you.

And so here we are, delving into exploring the power of PR, and the journey I'm taking you on is one of celebration, so you can learn how to truly celebrate you! Over the coming chapters you will start to see why this matters; why your story and experience must be shared and how PR opportunities are at your fingertips when you open up to them. When you start to believe you deserve to be celebrated, then, and only then, will you be able to make use of the practical tips in this book.

 The more you praise and celebrate your life the more in life there is to celebrate"

— OPRAH WINFREY

We are in for quite a ride as we explore the good, and the tricky parts of PR, but I want you to know that I'm already celebrating you and I want to thank you. I want to thank you, because you reading this book is already taking me a step further on my mission to empowering more female entrepreneurs to share their voices through me sharing what I know. You are already a part of a ripple effect, a legacy, and this is something to be celebrated! This stuff matters because if through this book I can encourage you to share your experiences, story, and expertise you can create a ripple effect that can have a global impact. A story is never just a story. To someone out there it will always be so much more.

So, thank you, really truly thank you, for buying this book, and here's to what we can achieve together- it's time to toast to what lies ahead!

It's time to prepare to *Celebrate You!* Cheers! Xx

———

Check In...

I know we haven't even got going yet but as I have learnt the power of self-reflection and self-awareness at a cost, I want to save you the heartache that comes with ignoring this stuff and just ploughing through.

Activity....

Write down how you are feeling right now - in bullet points, random words or full musings, it doesn't matter. What matters is to understand what your gut is telling you right now. How are you feeling about the path you are exploring here? Resistance, fear, excitement? A sense that you have something to share? Note it down so you can process it, be aware of it and reflect on it - and later we may challenge it. On we go x

2

ELEPHANTS IN THE ROOM

Ok and we're off. I've enticed you on this journey to exploring the fun we can have celebrating you...and I promise you PR provides so many different ways that you can do this. This should be an easy ride as celebrating is fun right?

I love a good party, the sound of popping Prosecco, old school tunes belting out, party games galore and drunken laughter....chuck in a cocktail fountain, some odd coloured party drinks and some fancy dress and I'm in heaven....these things make me happy. When I reminisce of times like this - be it my husband crawling along the floor dressed as a giant prawn one NYE morning in Abersoch; doing a three legged race on the Otley run when my sister took over Headingley with her geeks for her 30th birthday or my cousin (male) turning up to my Dad's 70th as Maggie Thatcher and belting out *'Man I feel like a woman'* in our back garden these memories literally make me beam from ear to ear, and they always will. They've been making me smile for years and I'm sure I'll continue to milk them for many years more! I can hear all the noises that go with these occasions and instantly feel the emotions attached to those events.

Memories are super powerful and good ones can really lift you when you need to dial into a bit of positivity or instant happiness.

I want you to think of your favourite party and zone right in. It's quite likely to be substantially cooler than my scenario (!) but go with your own version of events. Take a minute and just indulge in the fun of whatever is going on. How awesome does it feel to tap into that energy…? Of something being pure fun, of it being a bit playful, of you feeling so at ease and in the exact place you should be.

This is why I've chosen the theme of celebration for this book, because this is the energy that we are looking for because that air of celebration fills you with the big *whoop whoop* and the *let's do this* vibe.

celebrate

VERB

- acknowledge (a significant or happy day or event) with a social gathering or enjoyable activity
- honour or praise publicly

Celebrating is definitely fun, and I imagine you're pretty good at both of the above activities when it comes to momentous occasions, and celebrating other people's successes. But, how do you feel when you read those two definitions above when you put YOU at the heart of it? I know some of my friends don't even like having birthday parties because they don't want the day to be focused on them, I've even got a friend who hasn't got married because she doesn't like the thought of *'everyone staring at her'* as she walks down the aisle (to be fair I had a shot before I walked down the aisle so I do get where she's coming from but the appeal of the party after won me over!)

It's not uncommon to shy away from celebration when we attach it to meaning something else - perhaps to *'showing off'*, to *'ego'* to *'being full of it'* or *'liking being centre of attention'* - all things we're told as kids are bad.

The second definition, I imagine, might be the one that sits a bit heavier with you if you're not one for being centre of attention.

If this isn't you and you're all for it - big up to you, you'll go far! - but if the idea of someone wanting to *'honour or praise publicly'* something you have done, or have been through, or the idea of you being recognised and celebrated is something that makes you do an involuntary shudder, or indeed feel sick to the stomach then the rest of this chapter is for you.

Many of us do feel this way, me included, so it would be wrong of me if I just dived straight in here all gung-ho without addressing some of the challenges you might face when it comes to stepping up to become more visible - because I want to take this elephant out of the room.

When I talk about *Celebrating You* what I'm after is for you to step up and acknowledge ALL the stuff you have to share - be that sharing your story and dialling down into the elements which have been bumps in the road, (or indeed frigging enormous mountains to climb), which have led you to where you are today or whether it's recognising the huge power of your knowledge, acquired over your career, or life experience. This is the stuff that makes the lives of others better. This is the stuff that inspires others that they too can overcome a whole load of shit and that there's happiness to be had on the other side. This is the stuff that real impact is made of.

But it's not always easy.

Let me introduce you to Natalie. Natalie Anderson to be precise. A friend of mine who also happens to be a famous UK showbiz face, a much-loved actress, a familiar face reporting live on *This Morning*, a soap star from *Emmerdale* and *Hollyoaks*, and a blockbuster movie star alongside Liam Neeson & Guy Pearce. She's been nominated 'Britain's sexist woman' about a million times, is creatively multitalented and also respected as a singer and stage actress as well as her TV and film work - and she's a powerhouse businesswoman too who hosts a leading podcast and runs an incredible lifestyle brand, *The Capsule*.

Natalie is sweetest person you will ever meet. Kind, caring, unassuming she's kind of immune to the fact that she's drop dead gorgeous and is living a life many of us would dream of - but not in an arrogant way - far from it - she couldn't be less arrogant if she tried. It's more that she doesn't believe her own hype. She's a Yorkshire girl done good and is grateful for her every opportunity - she rocks the red carpet and 100% looks the part but deep down she finds it very hard to stand up and be celebrated. When she reads this is I KNOW she will already have cringed a million times about how I have introduced her and her accolades!

We have had many a conversation about the evil imposter syndrome which lies at the core of this (she joins other celebs such as Natalie Portman, Emma Watson and Helen Mirren who have openly discussed this), but one of the most interesting chats we've had has to be when she had just launched her business *The Capsule* and we were chatting over a wine about where she was taking it. She had created a gorgeous looking business - and in theory she had put her name to it – *The Capsule, by Natalie Anderson* - as she understood it made sense to use her recognition to support it - yet what she had effectively created was a faceless brand.

A beautiful brand, a gorgeously curated brand, but a faceless brand. What am I on about? Well, when Natalie told me about the reason she had set up *The Capsule* I was all in. I loved her passion, her connection to it, how it played out some child-hood dreams of wanting to work in fashion and beauty and how it was deeply connected to her own journey of anxiety and her exploration of products and services which had helped her though this.

She told me this over a wine. I connected with it, with her, with her mission. I was entranced. I was fascinated. I was invested in what she was producing.

She had not told me any of this on the website, in any of her content, or in any PR. I was a privileged trusted ally she had chosen to share this with. To the outside world *The Capsule* was just a pretty blog site that had cool products and some fun fashion advice......to me this was totally criminal as Jesus it was SOOOOO much more.

The elephant in the room was her story. A story she was scared to tell. A story she didn't want to consume her. A story she was fearful of being judged around. A story she hadn't yet owned.

And a story with so much power to help others.

Natalie believed that her anxiety was a weakness. She believed she'd be judged for it, scoffed for it, even dismissed because of it. She'd lose acting jobs, she'd be laughed at, she wouldn't be taken seriously in business because of it. There was for sure absolutely NO WAY she was going to hook her entire brand around it...of course she thought I was mad when I suggested she CELEBRATED it until.......she realised it would be wrong not to! She realised that she had to celebrate her journey, not shy away from it... she realised it was her duty to help others with what she'd learnt.... she realised that was the exact reason she'd set up her business.

She realised she needed to share it to let others into who she really was, to build trust with her audience, so she could then support them.

This didn't happen overnight, she resisted and resisted but then one day it became clear and what came next was amazing to watch.

She created a celebration. A celebration of her strength, a celebration of the support she'd received, a celebration of resilience, a celebration of women.

It was an 'in real life' event, where she decided to open up and remove the mask if you like. Isn't it weird that we feel the need to say it was 'in real life' these days after the Covid years?! - but this was a physical in the room event she had put together for her audience.

Natalie had told me:

> *"I love doing events and I love bringing people together, I love celebrating and showcasing others."*

This is what previous events had been around - giving others a platform to share their stories or sell their wares - but after our celebration conversation, this time she knew it had to be different, that she had to bring more of herself to the table to really connect. When I asked Nat to reflect on that game changing moment she said:

> *"Once the penny had dropped about owning my story, it felt like the right time to connect with my audience on a deeper level as I really wanted to start opening up deeper conversations around wellbeing and mental health and break down the stigmas around these issues - and I knew deep down that this*

*would be inauthentic if I continued to hide behind the mask of
my brand. How could I expect anyone to trust what I was
saying if they didn't know I'd been there myself?"*

She planned the event like any other but decided to use it as
an opportunity to face her own fears head on.

*"I added a slot into the evening where I shared my story - my
story of how anxiety had ruled me for years, of how I suffer
from imposter syndrome and I often feel out of my depth in
the world of business and the online space of entrepreneurship, of how I struggled with self worth and rejection and
how being an actress only fuelled this - then I shared the steps
I had taken to move myself through these challenges and
uphill struggles. I talked about my focus on wellbeing and
fitness, on mindfulness and breathing, of my commitment to
moving my body to help calm my mind. I shared techniques I
use and tools I have discovered that have helped me - I shared
the true essence of why I set up The Capsule."*

She went on:

*"What followed blew me away. In what was a very special
moment and one I will never forget, all of the audience
started to nod their heads in agreement at what I was
saying, turning to each other and saying 'that's me' to their
friends or even strangers. Some women started to share their
own stories and some just looked like a weight had been
lifted off their shoulders that they weren't alone....It really
was amazing, women of all ages, shapes and sizes united -*

united in a conversation around being imperfect, and in unspoken word they all promised to support each other, to empower each other, in knowing and emotionally fuelled glances they showed solidarity and understanding of each other. It was very special. And very emotional. This opening up of conversation, this feeling of being in a safe place where women could share their feelings without judgement, where they could admit to themselves things they had never really faced before was so so powerful. There were tears, there was laughter, and there was lots of hugging! - And for once, I also didn't feel alone, I saw that there were more women like me than I'd dared to believe... and then I felt fire, I didn't want so many women feeling bad about themselves in secret and silence and so it ignited even more passion than I had before. I felt more connected to the women I'd been trying to reach, I knew that my business actually had a real purpose and could be helpful and supportive in helping women build their confidence, protect their mental health and give them the tools to look after their overall wellbeing and it's these key factors that still drive me forward with The Capsule today."

This event and its outcome is a celebration that Natalie will remember forever. It's one she draws on to make her smile and likewise it's a moment all who were a part of will always remember too. Natalie has since incorporated her own mental health struggles in her PR, in content she writes and in conversations on her podcast where she interviews celebs about their own struggles too. Through all of this she has started to do her bit to removing the stigma around speaking honestly about mental health, she had helped others not feel alone, and she has inspired many thousands of people.

This is positive ripple effect, this is the power of celebration, the power of us sharing our triumphs of overcoming our fears. Pretty awesome right?

I felt the very fear that Nat felt when I first stepped into the online space. I was showing up as a PR expert and readily sharing my knowledge - however I wasn't bringing very much of me to the party - I wasn't celebrating my path that drove my passion, because I was too scared to let people in. I knew I was driven by the injustice of others not celebrating themselves and their amazing business and achievements and I felt passionately it was my duty to help more women in business to be seen, via the press, but in all honestly I actually didn't realise at first that this was due to my own imposter syndrome that had been stunting me - that the injustice I had felt at having my voice squashed by a bullying boss who loved his sense of self-importance was what fuelled me.

When I opened up to a coach about this and about how I didn't feel good enough to compete at the level I had been introduced in at in the online space (I was instantly guest-experting globally for the likes of Boss Babe and Niyc Pidgeon for example!) she mirrored back to me this was all self-worth issues. She made me realise I wanted to help other women who were stunting themselves because I was doing exactly that. She made me realise that I was driven to help other women who feel nervous about being visible - because I wanted to help them overcome the barriers, I had put in front of myself. More importantly she helped me realise the ONLY way I could help these women was to be honest with them, and myself. To open up and share the fact that I was a PR scared to be PR-ed, that I am someone with twenty years' experience in my field but suffer from imposter syndrome. She made me do this kicking and screaming because I thought it would jeopardise my professionalism, I thought it would turn people off. I thought I had to be perfect to be trusted. And I HATED the idea of sharing such personal feelings to those who already knew me but knew none of this about me. How wrong was I? As SOON as I started to be open and honest about how I felt I attracted attracted attracted. I attracted my ideal clients. I created the most incredible programmes from the heart, led by intuition of what those I wanted to help needed and I found incredibly powerful ways to guide them to get visible with confidence.

If I hadn't dared to be seen as who I really was I wouldn't have found this path.

If Natalie hadn't dared to share her story driving 'The Capsule' she wouldn't have built such a well-loved brand.

If you don't face your fears and connect with your own personal reasons for doing what you're doing you'll never reach your full potential... and neither of us want that!

Check In...

Make a note here of the three things that you are the most scared of when it comes to sharing your story or expertise by getting visible in the press. For some it's judgement, for some it's being 'found' out for being 'a fraud', for some it's that the media will not be interested and they fear rejection, perhaps its fear of how the info will be portrayed? What things come up for you? Let's face them head on

1. Being disliked
2. Having to show emotion
3. Someone discrediting my account.

Also see if you identify with this definition of Imposter Syndrome.

NOUN

imposter syndrome (*noun*)

- the persistent inability to believe that one's success is deserved or has been legitimately achieved as a result of one's own efforts or skills

When you're at the point to start taking action with your PR and if these fears start to raise their ugly heads have a listen to this episode on *PR Powerhouse* where I talk about how PR can actually help you overcome Imposter Syndrome. Let's bat away those fears and objections!

https://podcasts.apple.com/gb/podcast/pr-powerhouse-with-jo-swann/id1585138279?i=1000535494630

⚡ **Connect...**

Connect with Natalie Anderson and The Capsule via;

https://www.instagram.com/natjanderson/ and

https://www.instagram.com/officialcapsule/ and

https://podfollow.com/the-capsule-in-conversation/view

3

LET'S GET THIS PARTY STARTED

I n this chapter we're going to start to remove some of the mystery around PR because not many people enjoy venturing into the unknown and I get that PR can feel a bit scary because it is largely unknown, some even say a 'dark art'!

I don't like not knowing the score. I don't like turning up to a party where I don't know what to expect - I like to know the dress code, who will be there, the rough plan for the event, will there be food? Will there be dancing? My fave kind of parties are when I totally know the *'Party Promise'* so I can fully buy into the vibe. I know I'm kind of a special case! So in this chapter I'm going to fill you in a bit more on what you can expect from your PR Party...What exactly is on the cards? What's the promise? But first let's start with what you already think you know about PR.

"PR is for celebrities to flirt with the press."
"PR is for brands to manipulate their image."
"PR is for 7 figure business owners to celebrate making millions."
"PR is for charities or not for profits to fundraise."
"PR is for campaigning or rallying for a cause."
"PR is for corporate spin or reputation management."

Yes, it can be.

I'm not going to argue with you. PR can be all of those things.

PR is actually defined as:-

public relations

[public relations]

NOUN

- the professional maintenance of a favourable public image by a company or other organisation or a famous person.

To be honest I think this feeds many of the negative connotations of what PR is.

PR can be attached to the good the bad and the ugly - but I want you to forget about the bad and the ugly because when we talk PR in this book - and anywhere else you hear me talking PR we're talking PR for Good and we're talking about MUCH more than just maintaining a favourable public image. We're also talking about it in a wider sense than it just being used by big organisations, we're talking about using PR as actual real people connecting to actual other real people, on a human-to-human level. Jeees I think my new mission might have to be to get the dictionary definition rewritten!

For me

- PR is for sharing stories that help show there's hope
- PR is about celebrating people making a difference with their skills
- PR is about showcasing success of changemakers to inspire
- PR is about showing people they are not alone in their struggles
- PR highlights there can be light at the end of a very dark tunnel
- PR provides the tools to help others progress
- PR launches businesses in style
- PR builds businesses in super speed
- PR increases the value of your brand and sale price of your business
- PR opens doors to opportunities you never knew existed
- PR enables you to make your story count
- PR helps you change lives
- PR helps you save lives

Now that's pretty epic right? So, let's ditch PR's bad rep and give it the credit it deserves as a platform to empower change, to educate, to motivate and inspire. Let's celebrate how it helps us connect human to human. It's a seriously kick ass form of communications - and that's an important word to remember here too.

Communication. This is how I want you to think about PR. I want you to consider PR as a two-way conversation - a way of you discussing, and debating views, sharing experiences and knowledge with a view to opening up new thoughts and light-bulb moments for those who read your content.

PR is about storytelling, and we all know the power of story-telling - it's an age-old communication method valued throughout history.

Taking this out of PR context for a minute let's consider how we are connected to storytelling in our everyday lives.

When we go to the pub we share stories - this is what we do as humans, this is how we connect and communicate, this is how we catch up, how we celebrate, how we grieve or how we ask for help. Music is another form of storytelling we buy into. We buy into the lyrics, the message of the music because we connect with the stories being shared by the artists who are sharing their journey. This can feel empowering, cathartic, emotional and uplifting as we share the rollercoaster with the person who is opening up and being vulnerable.

This is effectively all PR right? – these are all examples of people choosing what to share with others to spread a certain message or evoke a certain reaction, or get a certain conversation going....

So PR rocks agreed? - yes yes and 100% yes! It's clever, it's subtle, it's crazy powerful.

So now let's tackle whether or not you think it's for you?

I want you to stop thinking about PR being *'for someone else'* and get used to realising that PR CAN be for you. Little old you. You working alone in your back bedroom or from your kitchen table, juggling the kids, and running a home alongside your entrepreneurial rollercoaster - wondering how the hell you do it all and sometimes why you do it all - then you remember you are driven by passion and purpose. You might be running a remote team, taking zoom calls in your gym gear, and managing all social media platforms in between trans-forming lives - but you ARE transforming lives with the work you do - you are making a difference to the quality of people's lives with your services or products. You are making an impact.

PR is here to celebrate you and all you have achieved, and will go on to achieve. It's here to showcase you and the difference you are making to your clients' lives. It's here to attract those ideal clients who would scramble over hot coals to get to what you can offer them if only they knew you existed. It's here for you.

But I don't expect you to fully believe me just yet, largely because PR is one of those industries that's shrouded in 'magic' - a bit like SEO or Facebook ads - the dark arts of the inter web! PR is similarly misunderstood because it's not a mainstream skill. It's a form of communication that is deemed a mystery to those 'outside of it'.

When we're talking about PR in this book, we are talking very specifically about media focused PR - we are talking about getting in the press - for free - and about using PR to celebrate and inspire. We'll go on to look at the rules of the game around this in a minute, because here's the first lesson - PR is about playing the game.

When you see peers or mentors featured in the press, do you wonder how they've done it? Do you presume they've been plucked from obscurity, researched by journalists, and then pinpointed for a feature? Wow they've made it - they've been noticed.

Newsflash. It very rarely happens this way. I'm sorry to burst your bubble but often even the *Top Ten Product recommendations*, *Top Ten Places to visit* and indeed *Top Ten Coaches* lists... are not necessarily the top ten. Shocker! They are the top ten the journalists KNOW about. They are the top ten that have got under the journalist's noses. They are the top ten who have provided the most useful media ready info and strongest images that will make their pages look good.

To get featured in the press for free you have to earn your place. You've got to play the game according to the journalists' rules to obtain that all important super valuable exposure in their publications.

An important thing to remember when you are embarking on your PR journey - *PR is a privilege not a rite of passage* - because to have PR success you have to respect it.

There are many false narratives about the industry in the media being that PR is a simple job that is more glamour than substance; that it's all about champers and parties and being *Fabulous Darling* but PR when done right has SO much more depth, and so much power to skyrocket businesses and brands to the next level than all that. Don't get me wrong I love the parties and champers (as you already know!) But I love them the most when we're celebrating your success not some superficial bollocks from a big corporate which we've managed to turn into a PR story. I've been responsible for a lot of that in my time and it's not something I want to be a part of anymore. These days I am proud of what we use PR for. I am proud of the incredible women we get to champion, cheerlead and showcase - and the stories we get to share.

Coming back to stories again and playing the game - how do stories lead to your PR success? Well, here it helps if we look at what PR is NOT just as much as considering what it is.

You know when you're organising a party and you have to think about who to invite - and not to invite, you make decisions on the best fit, don't you? You won't necessarily invite someone who will clash with everyone else, go around shouting their mouth off and generally being a bit brash and in your face?

Well in the PR world this is *'Advertising'*. Advertising and its friend Sales are not invited to the PR Party. They are not welcome, they are not liked, they will be thrown out make no mistake! Now I'm not saying there's zero place for advertising or sales as part of your wider marketing mix - that would be crazy - but there is most definitely not a place for it at the PR Party.

Public Relations is often mistaken for the same thing as advertising when it comes down to the marketing of your brand, because people simply don't understand the difference. But it's not hard to grasp when we consider that PR does exactly what it says on the tin 'public relations', it's essentially building up a stronger and more meaningful relationships with your desired public. It's connecting you on a very real level. It's about providing information that provides insights and value. Advertising doesn't do this.

This brings with it some interesting challenges - and if you've been used to using advertising to market your business you will be feeling very out of your comfort zone when it comes to PR - because the rules of the game are VERY different. To achieve PR success, you have to tick the boxes of what the journalists want and need - stories - to play the game that can result in you achieving free press coverage.

You've got to *'Story tell not Sell!"* Please repeat this a million times. Write lines on it. Have it tattooed on your hand - it's SO essential!

When advertising is paid for and brands pay for space in a newspaper, or a magazine to directly promote to the audience they (within reason and the ASA guidelines) can say what they like. They can sell what they like. They can add whatever links and pricing info they like.

But when PR is free and you are generating earned media not bought media there's a different dynamic at work. This way round you are in need of the journalist to publish your info, you are in need of their buy in, and what they need are stories. People stories, stories of resilience, topical stories, stories of adversity and diversity, stories that inspire and motivate supported by knowledge sharing that brings value upon value.

They don't want much do they? What's next - blood?!

What you have to remember is that journalists are bound by editorial practice guidelines and industry regulations - it is not their job to promote your business for free. It is not their job to shove your business goods and services down the throat of their readers - it is their job to share stories and knowledge - and as it happens this is what your audience wants too. Your PR might focus around your story, or it might be around your knowledge sharing - there is no one style of PR party - but they all abide by the same rules.

Storytelling marketing has increased significantly over the last couple of years as people crave connection and community, post Covid isolation. You're probably already doing this in your social posts - so why not via the media too? Because it seems scarier when the press is involved, bigger somehow. I get it. But it doesn't have to be so scary when you understand it.

Some of the world's most renowned entrepreneurs hold PR in high esteem. Richard Branson famously said that *"PR is infinitely more effective than a front-page advert"* and Bill Gates is on record saying, *"If I was down to my last dollar of marketing, I would spend it on PR"*. Two of the most successful people in the world both have glowing opinions on PR. Why - because of the power of its third-party endorsement - getting others to shout about them is actually way more powerful than them shouting about themselves - (and it's significantly cheaper too!)

Let's look at this a different way and consider the power of influence in this scenario.....

If a young man tells his date, how young and smart and successful he is, that's advertising. If a young man tells his date, she's intelligent and she looks lovely and is a great conversationalist he's saying the right things to the right person and that's marketing. If someone else tell the young women how smart and successful, her date is then that's PR (S. H. Simmons)

There is no better advertising than word of mouth and this is where PR comes in.

Making sense? I hope so!

So, revisiting the PR Promise, and considering what it's bringing to the party I'd like to offer you:-

- Visibility
- Credibility; and
- Connection

Combined with a hefty sprinkling of :-

- Brand Ownership
- Business Growth; and
- INCREDIBLE Impact.

Fancy some of that?

Now you're feeling a little more at ease around what to expect from your PR party are you excited to go? It's time to get fired up about the fun you can have with it.

4

ECSTASY - OH WHAT A FEELING!

So here we are. You now know that PR is based around stories, and storytelling, yes?, and everyone loves a good story right? - so let's dive into just how incredibly powerful stories can be and how sharing them can make us feel.

Stories make us laugh, stories make us cry, stories give us hope, stories make us think.

I have just watched a film that was telling a real-life story about a man who walked across America, after his gay son took his own life. He was walking thousands of miles to speak to anyone who would listen and spread the message of the dangers of bullying, asking people to think about the impact words have on others. This film was shocking, it was full of emotion - it was full of sadness, it was full of regret, it was full of reflection, but I loved it. I loved it because it felt real, I loved it because it made me cry, I loved it because I saw into the soul of the characters, their pain, their love, their struggles. I loved it because it followed the journey of a man who had something to say and a message to spread that intended to galvanise change, and he was determined to make his words count. I loved it because it showed the honest journey of someone who struggled with his own emotions, and who recognised his flaws and was trying to put them right, it showcased someone healing, who was trying to do better, to be better, for the sake of honouring his son, but also for the sake of being a positive, not negative, ripple effect - it also showed someone laying themselves on the line…for their own healing journey.

I loved it for all those reasons, and I also loved it because Mark Wahlberg was in it - well these things always help! - but aside from the fact he's a treat on the eye- his presence, his lovability and his 'rawness' (I'm not sure that's even a word but you know what I mean) all played into the success of the film. I liked him, I connected with his character, flaws and all.

I hated the end as it felt like a trauma too far - but it was a real-life story and that doesn't always have a happy ending, does it?

Your story has a happy ending though. The fact you are here today reading this book means your story has a happy ending. The fact you are ready to be a voice for change, or a champion of others, or a knowledge sharer, an educator, a mentor or coach means you get to also give others happy endings.

This is incredible.

The power of stories should never be underestimated. The power of connecting to people on a human to human level should never be underestimated. Stories enable evolution. Stories enable cultural change. Stories break damaging generational cycles. Stories change lives.

I've seen stories change lives right in front of my very eyes. Stories that inspire and motivate people to make change, having seen someone else do it, having overcome similar challenges.

I've seen women who've experienced trauma, as a result of sexual abuse, find their confidence again and rise from their feelings of shame and unworthiness, to start to feel empowered and in control of their lives again - because they've followed the journey of someone who's celebrated this.

I've seen women move away from dangerous relationships which kept them trapped, walk away, feeling strong thanks to being fuelled by stories of others' triumphs.

I've seen women who were hiding their mental health challenges, fighting them alone, often to a point where they are in the darkest of places, RISE, rise to get help, rise to talk about the unspeakable, rise to support others suffering.

I've seen women quit lifelong careers that were making them depressed and anxious make a change to follow their passion and purpose, after seeing this is possible, it's not just for the movies!

I've seen women drowning in debt find a way out and create a new path for themselves that gives them financial freedom -

after taking the first step provided for free, by someone who's been there and come out the other side and is now on a knowledge sharing mission.

It's INCREDIBLE what I've seen via the ripple effect of PR. Often our clients get messages from readers thanking them for having shared their story, saying how inspired they are, saying how much they've appreciated the honesty, and often asking *'are you in my head? - because this is exactly what I needed to hear'*.

Just imagine this for a second. You've written an article in a magazine you massively respect, maybe one you've grown up with, or maybe a prestigious one in your field - it's about your journey, your struggles, your challenges - that you have now overcome. It shares your story, your learnings, your knowledge and offers a friendly supportive hand on the shoulder for someone who is where you were. You offer empathy and understanding, and actionable tips on small steps they could take to start moving themselves forward today.

You get an email, a ping on your What'sApp, a Facebook message, a call from someone who simply says, *'Thank you'*. Thank you for being brave. Thank you for daring to share. Thank you for choosing to inspire. What would this mean? The feeling of purpose, the feeling of being seen, of being recognised -it's quite something - something we often don't realise we need but so many of us do (especially if we are born people pleasers). This feedback feeds us, drives us and our focus, it fuels us and validates our work. Yes I did say validates our work - and I don't say that lightly as I know constantly striving to be validated by someone else is not a healthy thing and of course we shouldn't need this to feel successful - BUT if this IS a need of yours (I don't mind admitting it is one of mine), if contribution is a big deal for you, then this just feels so powerful.

It feels BLOODY AMAZING! This is a natural high that honestly feels like nothing else. It speaks to your soul. It connects to your emotions on SOOOO many levels - it's like all the good stuff and none of the bad stuff of illegal highs - and there is no come down! In fact, is usually just keeps getting better.

ecstasy
NOUN

- an overwhelming feeling of great happiness or joyful excitement.

When you are able to make people feel like this you are connected! When you feel like this you are driven like never before.

Often following such a connection, and feeling such heightened emotions people want more. Of course we do - it's a natural instinct, so when your ideal clients have consumed and loved your PR this is often followed by - *'how can I work with you?'* - so you get the added bonus of it being income generating - enabling you to grow your business from a place of passion and purpose - but don't forget, this only works if you have been fully focused on your purpose in the first place.

One of our clients, Hannah, who you'll meet later in the book, became booked up within weeks of working with us, as her PR was speaking to her exact ideal client, niched right down to be speaking their language, and holding a mirror to show them who they are but also who they could be. Her raw honest story pinpointed and connected her to her dream clients - and it can do this for you too.

There is always someone where you were. There is always someone who needs hope that they can leave there - that they can move on, that there is something else, something better, at the other side for them... but how do they get to the other side? They need guiding there. They need handholding. They need inspiring.

What a bloody great job to do for someone. What a frickin' awesome role to play in someone's life. Yes please - count me in!

I'm all for this responsibility. And it is a responsibility - I honestly do see it like that. That those of us who have learnt life lessons, no matter how big or small, come out the other side and throw back a helping hand for others, a hand that others can grab, a hand that can help others rise up. This is what my amazing client and friend Dani Wallace does. Dani's brand is 'I am the Queen Bee' and her mantra is 'show up, wise up, rise up'. As a mentor and public speaking coach - and someone who's been through domestic abuse, homelessness, desertion, debt...she has set the bar for herself to prove to others what's possible – no matter where you start out. She talks about this as being an inner desire, something she can't fight, something that literally pushes her out of bed in a morning - it's in her very being.

Her *'I am the Queen Bee'* movement is about empowering others to claim their birth right of success and happiness - it's really not even about her. Throughout the growth of her business over the last few years she has ALWAYS put that hand out to help others up, every single step of the way - from creating a free online talk show in lockdown that provided connection, community and guidance and helped others improve their mental health at a really difficult time, to creating an epic celebrity charity chat-a-thon which raised over £16K for domestic violence charities, to setting up her own charitable foundation - The Fly Anyway Foundation, to support survivors of domestic abuse to set up their own businesses, to start to rebuild their lives and create financial independence. This woman walks the walk and it's a total joy to be celebrating her through the PR as she goes. To use the power of PR to inspire and motivate as many people as possible, for me, is giving PR its true purpose in life and to witness first-hand the direct impact this storytelling and knowledge sharing has on the people it reaches is something truly special.

Someone else who believes wholeheartedly in the power of storytelling is American singer and songwriter Demi Lovato - now I am unable to boast that she is our client (but wouldn't that be cool?) – however, I'm quite sure she won't mind me referencing her here. I looked her up recently after she's put some songs out that attracted lots of attention, I was really intrigued about how powerful her language was in her songs. She is very open and honest about how much of herself she puts into her songs, and she talks about how her song writing has been a bit of a journey of love and confidence. You can see that when you look back at all the things that she's written. You can see her journey - you can really get to know her as an individual, as a person and a lot of her lyrics really show her strong and her vulnerable side. She's very much about sharing her story to inspire and to empower others informing us about her journey and helping us connect with that, so that we can find hope to come out the other side of our own struggles. I think she's a really interesting person when you're thinking about storytelling, because one of the things that she also says is she wears her lyrics, *"like a badge of honour"*.

I love that quote. I love it. How cool is that? She is basically saying I am using my songs as a timeline of my life. I'm using my songs as a way of recording what was happened to me, as a badge of honour of what I've been through and what I've achieved, celebrating how I've managed to come out the other side. I think that is a really, really powerful way to think about it. Using your story and using language to communicate what you've learned, what you've been through and think about how that can help other people. Demi Lovato is very much an artist that is aware of her influence. And she's very much an artist who is aware of all of her power and the power that her words can have on other people.

She says:

> *I learned the power of storytelling and the responsibility that people with influence have to speak out."*
>
> — DEMI LOVATO

Now, I just want you to think about that for a minute, particularly that last part, the responsibility that people with influence have to speak out.

Steve Jobs says:

> *The most powerful person in the world is the storyteller."*
>
> — STEVE JOBS

That can be you. YOU can be that storyteller. YOU can make a difference to other people's lives as well as your own. YOU can through the power of PR.

So are you in? Who are you going to inspire? What do you want to do with your story?

Your story counts in the here and now. Your story, whilst potentially painful to share, could bring you so much joy, because of its power, because of the ripple effect it could create.

Fancy feeling all the feels of it changing someone's life? Right then, let's think about *your* story and the work it can do.

✦ *Activity....*

Jot down the parts of your story you think you might need to share, to help your audience take inspiration and motivation from your journey.

Early years / Family Upbringing:

→ new age traveller

→ murder.

→ drugs and alcohol.

→ Ireland > Brighton > Wales.

→ Education + morals.

→ Dad + cancer.

→ Matriarchal family.

Career path / Corporate World:

Crunch 3 - 60 people.

Unicorn + ACME - O - Z + M.

Media Week 30 v 30.

Board Director at 27

Media week awards.

Leading three agencies by 30.

Adversity / Challenges:

Working 1 trillion hours.

Losing #1m clients.

Sacking a blind person.

Becoming part of a wider group.

Being young + female in a male enviro

Lightbulb/Defining Moments :

___

When I backed myself over company.
Being told 'I thought i was very good!'
Realising that aged 30 - I'd set up 3 film agencies
Working 1 freelancer + 2 jobs > but only paid for one.
Realising i had stopped learning

___

Other:

___

___

___

___

___

___

___

___

___

⚡ Connect...

Connect with Dani, I am The Queen Bee Movement and The Fly Anyway Foundation via

https://www.facebook.com/thequeenbeedani and

https://www.instagram.com/thequeenbeedani/ and

https://www.instagram.com/flyanywayfoundation/ and

https://www.iamthequeenbee.co.uk/

5

GET PARTY PLANNING!

Ok strap yourself in - this chapter is a biggie and it needs you to think! Get yourself a cuppa, a glass of wine, a stash of sweets, or a gorgeous candle... whatever works to get you in the zone, as we dive into party planning your PR success!

I always wanted to be a party planner. As I might have already mentioned, I love a good party - my kids love a good party, my whole family loves a good party - it's a trait I'm determined keeps getting passed down through the generations. I love the fun of a party, the playfulness of it, but I love it the most when I'm in control of it!

This is something someone once commented on that I love to be the, *'Queen of organised fun'* - and it's true! Don't get me wrong, I love turning up to a party and diving into whatever's going on but if it's my party or my kid's party or my friend's Hen do there's an adrenaline rush of anticipation and expectation for weeks, sometimes months before, that I thrive on! I become obsessed with all the little extras I could throw in, what surprises could I organise, what theme are we having (there has to be a theme!), what decor do we need... the list goes on. And one thing always at the centre of my mind is celebration - celebration of whoever the party is for, or whatever occasion it is representing. In all the parties I plan, I make sure there is a real opportunity to celebrate that person or occasion in full glory.

Shining a light on others is defo my bag, and maybe this is a part of that, but when the day comes, I thrive on people enjoying themselves, enjoying the experience, and the escapism that brings.

You will find all this out if you ever come to any of our events as I take the same approach with all we do within Chocolate PR too. Our events are fun, memorable and most defo party like - but they also have a purpose.

As PR coaches myself and my team guide our clients on the path they should take. They look to us for direction, for guidance on how they can engage with the media in a way that makes sense to their end goal. Good PR is not knee-jerk, it's not the reactive stuff done in isolation (getting a quote in here and there thanks to a 'journo request' is great as part of a bigger picture but isn't a strategy in its own right - more on that later if you don't know what I'm talking about). It's about thinking long-term, it's about having a plan of what your end goal is - and understanding how you want to make people feel along the way.

Being in PR is much like being a party planner and I want you to start thinking about being the party planner of your own life now.

It's time to *Celebrate You* - so how are we going to do that? What's going to be involved? What vibe do we want? What tone do we want to set? What are the exciting extras going to be?

It's task time. I'm going to ask you some random, and what may seem superficial meaningless questions, but these are questions we ask our Mastermind clients who sign up to work with us for six months as part of their induction session when we are getting under their skin. Answer them intuitively and it will be interesting to reflect on what you find.

1. What drink would you be and why? *cappucino - gets you going, strong, fluffy top*
2. What chocolate bar would you be and why? *Galaxy - smooth, high end.*
3. What superpowers would you have and why? *invisibility cloak.*
4. What celebrity would you be and why? *Jaro Blakely - fun, focused & results driven.*

As an example of how this works here are some of the findings we took from our clients undertaking this exercise…

Their answers were:-

1. A glass of sparkly Prosecco
2. A chilli flavour Green & Blacks
3. X-ray vision
4. Helen Mirren

Ok, all very fun, but where do we go from there? How do we use this to then craft our PR path, to plan our own PR party, to celebrate us?

What we discovered from this playful exercise upon further discussion having got them to tap into their characteristics was that:-

1. They want to be seen as fun and bubbly, bringing the sparkle.
2. They bring a cheeky and surprising edge, but overall a high-quality premium experience.
3. One of their qualities is to really see people, see into their inner feelings and thoughts and they are told often that they see through people's masks.
4. They are no nonsense, straight talking, confident and assertive, embracing life experience and knowledge.

All these realisations helped to paint a picture of how this person needs to show up - if they want to authentically connect via their true qualities and values and attract like-minded clients who will adore them.

The point you see is around celebrating YOU - the real you, the possibly hidden you, the unfiltered version of you, the YOU that's driven by your true character, your very essence, and it's quite likely you're not doing this. This is because often when we start out in business, or enter a new world like the online space, we create a 'fake I.D' governed by marketing spiel, or copywriters or an outdated brand identity we knocked up years ago. We sit (read 'hide') behind this as it feels safe and relatively comfortable. Sooooo many of the women who first come to us are doing this - they are not showing up as them - not really, some not at all.

I didn't show up as me when I first entered this online space. Yes, you saw a bit of me, yes you got a sense of my character, to a degree - because I can't do fake personas, so you did get me - but you didn't get all of me - you really didn't get let in very much, you didn't get the chance to get to know me or truly connect with me unless you were already in my circle. I was hiding, hiding behind a mask of 'professionalism' of what I thought I should look like to be respected (because I felt out of my depth having moved into the glamorous female focused online world from a bricks and mortar business world where I networked mostly with men). In this new world I was unsure of myself and where I fit in, and so I was leaving a WHOLE lot out! I felt late to the party and on the back foot. I still found my people as eventually you do, but I didn't make it easy for myself or them and I wasted a hell of a lot of time - HUGELY frustrating! I also felt hugely misaligned, I felt stuck, I felt like I was swimming against the tide, and I felt like an imposter trying to make her name in a new world, but what really was that name? You see if you don't go all in with you, you can't fully show up, and when you can't fully show up you do things by halves, when you do things by halves you don't achieve the success you desire - and when that happens you feel like a failure, no matter what you are actually achieving. This was me.

The thing that changed everything for me - apart from taking the leap to invest in a damn good coach (the amazing Andrea

Callanan) was when I got back to my core mission. I started to ask myself why I was here in the first place? Why had I turned my back on a very lucrative business model of working with big retainers with big brands to join the online space and work with individuals who often didn't have anywhere near those budgets? Why?

Because I was unhappy. Because I was angry. Because I was sad.

I quit working with big corporates because I hated the lack of control I had, because my creativity was stunted, I felt trapped and not able to be me, my values were compromised, and I was done with being treated like someone's minion who was expected to follow the lead being forced down a very agenda-based path even though they had chosen to invest in my creative consultancy.

I totally reworked by business to incorporate PR coaching into it because I truly believe its criminal that so many small business owners are not capitalising on the 'leveller' PR can be - because they are scared of it, or in awe of it, choosing to believe it's not for them, when it could be a fundamental tool to catapulting their business growth. When I came across incredible women doing incredible things having quit successful corporate careers to run a mission led business, I wanted to help them. Their stories were so powerful, and their businesses deserved to succeed not fail (which is what would happen if they stayed invisible!)

I am on a knowledge sharing mission to help more small businesses and female entrepreneurs see that PR CAN be for them, and not just the big boys, because I want to help others fight imposter syndrome so it doesn't stunt their growth like it did for me.

ALL of these things matter to me, really matter, and it was when I connected back to that, with the help of Andrea, everything made so much more sense. She got me to open up about my imposter syndrome - after various crying episodes when I let her in. This was something I'd never openly recognised before - and sure as damn it I wasn't going to start publicising the fact I felt like this - a PR who wasn't happy PR-ing herself - doesn't seem quite right does it? She helped me to see that this vulnerability would be exactly what would attract my dream clients, she made me see that in sharing this I would become a magnet to people I wanted to help - others who were fearful about being visible just like me.

So, from here - I started again. Not from scratch with the business, but if you followed me on social media you would defo have noticed an invisible line. I stopped being scared of not being liked by everyone. I focused on my mission and purpose and I used that to guide my path.

I created my first online programme - *Dare to Be Seen* - which really spoke to other female entrepreneurs who were hiding. The programme guides and handholds you through being scared to be seen to daring to be seen with all the steps in between, from overcoming imposter syndrome (with Andrea as our guest expert) to connecting to your story to understanding how the media works, to getting published in the national media - all just in eight weeks. We push and guide you with love, and arm you with everything you need to be media ready no matter how much of a PR novice you are and how out of your comfort zone getting published feels like. I ADORE this programme and it came from the heart. With a blend of coaching, mindset and PR training it really is a winning formula and the clients who have been through it fly. Dani (aka The Queen Bee) was one of our first graduates, and just look at her go!

After this the next thing I rolled out in the business was our 'Get in the Press- Live!'- membership - this ticked a box for me on my mission as it filled the gap of supporting people who couldn't afford our other services - you see I want to help everyone and was feeling out of sorts that unless I became a charity I couldn't actually do this! So, the membership is a low-cost way to get into our world, and to tap into PR opportunities. Clients have found their feet in here and celebrated being featured in national press - magic defo happens even on a small budget.

More recently came our 'More Than Media - Make Me Famous Mastermind' - this was born from a realisation that I had so much wider experience from working with all the big brands that I wasn't using in our other programmes, and it felt like a waste. It also came from my desire to help ambitious female entrepreneurs really level up and fully own their space, not just through press but through awards and campaigns and collaborations etc. I love the opportunity to spend six months with them to really create robust strategies - this has been game-changing for some very special women.

Last year (2021) I really stepped into spreading my message further and wider - again to the masses, and I found the Podcast route as a way to reach even more people - who could access my advice for free - this felt so good! *PR Powerhouse* was launched and charted as a No.1 in launch week, and it still sits within the top 2% of podcasts globally - mind-blowing!

This brings us to this book.

In sharing those key business developments, I hope you've seen how I've grown the business to further fuel my own mission and goals and that also if you follow me I hope that you will also see that whilst doing so I have stayed true to my brand identity that I have now owned of being a fun playful, approachable brand.

My business growth was driven by my core 'Authority Goal': *"I want to empower more female business owners' voices to be heard, especially those who feel nervous about being seen, because I truly believe in the power of storytelling and knowledge sharing to change lives. It's my mission to make PR accessible to more small business owners and to change the landscape of the media so that more diverse voices are celebrated"*.

Being so clear on this driver has kept me on track. I want you to connect to yours now.

YOUR AUTHORITY GOAL

It's time to connect to the emotion behind what you do and why you do it, so you can create your own party plan aka your PR path. It's a case of being super clear about what your mission is and what change you want to make with your work, so you can proactively head towards achieving that. PR is a fabulous tool for illustrating you walking your walk - but you have got to know what walk you are walking first!

An *Authority Goal* is a term we have created to help our clients clearly define the goal they are working towards with their mission, and more specifically what commitment they are making as part of this. When you are super clear on what this is it is a million times easier to see where your PR focus should lie - what content you should share, what parts of your story you need to celebrate.

I'd love you to ask yourself these questions as a route to gaining clarity on your *Authority Goal* because it needs to be driven by passion and purpose.

- What makes you angry? *People that bring bad energy.*
- What makes you cry? *Hopelessness for family.*
- What gives you hope? *Young people.*
- What change do you want to make? *Support young people to make a difference.*

This exercise is inspired by a creative marketeer called Todd Henry who refers to the above as 'your notables'.

Once you take time to really take stock of the things that matter to you then your path becomes so much clearer, because it relates to you taking action to make a change in the areas you have identified above.

It's no good me just sitting bitching at a dinner party that I want to see more underrepresented voices in the media, whinging that it gets me cross that the large media outlets make it really difficult for smaller businesses to have a voice. It's no good me just daydreaming to my friends that things could be different and wouldn't it be fabulous to see more small business owners - especially women - who work part time around their kids, be represented in the national media as 'proper business people' - rather than being referred to as 'kitchen table businesses' or 'side hustles.' Sharing these views purely in my own circles is not constructive to creating change, not big change.

To create big change, I need to take considered action to influence.

To create big change, I need to be focused on spreading my message in places of impact.

To create big change, I need to bring others with me.

To create big change, I need to commit to a PR pathway.

You CANNOT create change alone - however much you might feel inspired to try. When you have the right 'team' you are always stronger together - and those team members could be your staff, your clients, your audience.

To create change you often have to lead. When you are someone driven so passionately by something it's your responsibility to galvanise others. It's your job to send the invites to the party out so that others CAN come along for the ride, and bring their skills to the table too, but often you have to create that path for others to follow.

Go back to your *Authority Goal* and breathe it in. Breathe in the importance of it, the power of it, the impact it will make if you achieve it.

Now let's party plan your route to that.

WHAT PARTY ARE YOU INVITING PEOPLE TO?

What is it called? What can people expect from this party? What will they love about it?

So this is about being able to clearly communicate your mission and the end result you are looking for - so for Dani - she is inviting people as part of the Queen Bee Movement to *'Show up, Wise Up and Rise Up'* so they can live their best lives, whatever that means to them, encouraging them to be a positive influence on the world around them at the same time. She's inviting people to reclaim their birth right of success. She's inviting people to take hold of their challenges, to recognise them and respect them, but then inviting them to choose to *fly anyway*. People can expect to be inspired, motivated and empowered if they join this party. They will love the sense of community, fun and solidarity.

What can people expect from joining you? When you know the answer to this, this is a thread that runs through your PR via your core mission message.

How do you invite them? What kind of invite do you use? What do they look like? How is your invitation communicated? What's the vibe?

So here we're looking at your character and tone - would your invites be bold, bright and brave in tone and language? Or would they be sleek, sophisticated and softer in language? We're also looking at medium - would your guests prefer something digital or something in print in their hand, something creative or more straightforward? Whichever you choose will appeal to a different crowd, so think carefully about who you want to come to your party. What are the key words that are coming to mind that represent you and your style? What does this look like and feel like?

When you decide this, this is the tone and character that needs to run through your PR content.

WHO ARE YOU INVITING?

Is everyone invited or just a select few/niche audience? Are you intending to appeal to women, or all genders and a more diverse community? Knowing exactly who you are wanting to come to your party really helps you hone your communication to them

Who do you want at your party? (As clients or partners?) When you know make sure you speak directly to those people in your PR content.

WHERE IS THE PARTY?

Where can they join you and when?

What specific thing are you organising where people can come together and join forces? What 'happening' are you organising so you can bring 'your people' together? If there's no address people can't show up -and you're at your party all alone, crying into your cocktail, so think about what space you can create to host people.

In your business this may be a Facebook group, a summit, workshop or online festival, an in-person event, a charity fundraiser, a campaign activity for an awareness day. There are so many ways you can bring people together, but you do need something.

What can you do to drive people towards you, so they can join you and be a part of your mission? Ideally you want multiple ways, over a prolonged period of time as consistency is key and repetition brings reward - but what could work as your next step? Maybe you already have some of these things in place, so what would be a real crescendo that you could work towards to amplify your efforts?

WHAT'S THE 'MEMORABLE MOMENT'?

At every good party there's a memorable moment - often it is curated by the organiser as a highlight of the event (think photo booths, crazy dancing, competitions, entertainment) When you are the one in charge of the party it's your responsibility to provide these memorable moments - because if you're inviting someone along of the ride then you're in charge of that ride, as far as I see it.

PR is about communication, it's a two-way conversation between you and your reader and it's your job to make them feel something. Make them feel something that makes them want to be in your world. Make them feel something that they will forever connect to you.

So think about if you are reaching out to people to bring them with you on your mission, how do you want to leave them feeling as a result of the content they consume from you? What emotions do you want to evoke in them? Then make sure you call to these in your PR content.

WHAT'S IN THE PARTY BAG?

When the fun's been had then what? Then it's time to go home, back to our own worlds what happens then? We get packed off with our party bags as a reminder of what a great time we've just had, and as we eat the cake (or chocolates if you've been to a party of ours!) and smile a happy smile grateful for the fun.

So here think about how you want to have made people feel, after coming to your party? What is the impact you wish to have had had? How do you want them to fondly remember you? How do you want them to feel about you? What have you left them with to devour, chew on, or explore?

What's in your party bag?

Making sure you GIVE is important so that whether or not people come back for more you have provided value, you have improved their lives in some small way, so from a PR perspective be free and generous with your knowledge, resources and information that could help those you wish to help. They will remember you for it. They will love you for it. And they'll want to come back to your party.

Do you have a lead magnet you could point people towards at the end of a tips article for example? Having a lead magnet as your party bag gift is a gift that keeps on giving as you'll get to keep in touch over and over again and your new audience member will become fully immersed in your world.

⚡ *Activity....*

So how's your party planning going? Did that spark any ideas?

What's the mission you want people to join you on?
What's the vibe you want them to get?
Who is the ideal client you need to get in front of?
How will you make them connect with you and remember you?
What can you give them to help them love you more?

Jot your ideas down here:

_____

_____

_____

MISSION - PUT THE INNOVATION BACK INTO
MARKETING.

VIBE - FUN BUT FOCUSED. PREMIUM
BUT ACCESSIBLE. ENGAGING.

IDEAL CLIENT - GOOGLE, MBZUM.

HOW TO CONNECT - LI, EVENTS-
REMEMBER AS HIGHLY ENGAGING
& KNOWLEDGABLE

WHAT TO GIVE THEM - KNOWLEDGE.
GIFTS

6

RAISING THE ROOF

This chapter is all about making noise to get people talking now you're getting clearer about what it is you want to say. It's here to get you to think about standing behind your message proudly and with conviction. It's asking you to imagine standing on your soapbox and shouting out to the world what mission you're on.

If there's one thing I know about hosting a good party, it's that the vibe of the host is EVERYTHING. If you're shy and meek, hiding in the corner or half-heartedly suggesting people might like to do this or that then you're going to have people falling asleep in their canapés and running for the hills abruptly. A host must lead from the front. YOU must lead from the front.

So you have your mission. You're clear on the message you want to get out to the world. Now it's time to turn up the volume, not just one notch but several notches....it's time to raise the roooooooooof!

Ok, so how do we do this? I'm going to share one of our amazing clients with you, who has fiercely stepped into being an incredible host of her own PR party. She has taken what we've taught her and embraced it to the max, to make powerful impact with her work, and to really command her space through PR - despite being a total PR novice when we met.

Let's meet Louisa. Louisa Herridge, is a feisty fun loving character, who has overcome huge adversity which very nearly broke her true spirit, and which caused depression, anxiety and crippling self-doubt - but Louisa is also a global speaker, a best-selling author and the founder of kick ass brand *Mamas Ignited* and this is how Louisa describes herself today:

> *"I'm a mindset and positive psychology coach and best-selling author who inspires women who want to be more, do more and have more in life to ignite their spark so that they move away from their ironing boards, and instead ride their surfboards to create the success that they want in their lives and businesses, because a surfboard is just an ironing board who gave up on its dream and we all deserve better than that...."*

...ooo this sounds interesting right? Right! More about ironing boards and surfboards in a minute - but it's safe to say that Louisa is pretty darn confident about communicating her character, who she is and what she stands for?

Just over a year ago Louisa was a full-time teacher so this world of online entrepreneurship is a whole new world to her

- but it's one she's entered with gusto. I'll let her tell you in a nutshell, a little of her journey of her becoming who you see before you today.

Louisa:

"I was an English teacher for sixteen years and it was something I loved. I love teaching because I love my subjects and I am a writer and I love writing, but it came to me in a therapy session after I'd gone through a breakdown after leaving an abusive relationship, that I didn't have to be a teacher for the rest of my life....and that actually I had kind of 'ended up here'. And although I wasn't looking for an escape plan at that point, I had this spark in me to want to do more and be more myself.

When I look back now on my life and childhood (as Jo made me do as part of my story building process) I can see sooooo many signs that I was always destined for more. I can see my ambitious independent creative qualities oozing out of the younger more confident me, characteristics that for so long I buried after having them squished out of me at several different life changing moments - but characteristics I have totally reconnected with as the leader of Mamas Ignited.

So that's why I'm so passionate about my mission because I was that woman who had become trapped by life, by others, by following a path I thought I should follow and I did what I needed to do to release myself - but only after extreme trauma....I was pushed to breaking point and was in the darkest of times before I even thought about changing my life....and I don't want others to wait this long to live their true purpose.

Thanks to my personal development journey and mindset tools I recreated my life and made it one that now totally fills me with joy and purpose - an online business that works around me being a solo mum, through which I get to inspire other women. What's funny is that in the process, I've actually lived my dream out, which was publishing my own book. This year I have celebrated being a best-selling author of my own book and also being the person who brought together a collection of other incredible women with stories to share, in a collaboration book with another in the pipe-line. So from English teacher to published author, yep, that sounds pretty cool to me actually."

It's very cool and it's been amazing to watch Louisa do this and to really own her own dreams and aspirations, taking hold of these and making them happen. She decided that she was going to change direction, and use what she'd learnt on her personal development journey to support others - BUT Louisa didn't just start a business like some people just start a business, like kind of quietly in the corner, under the radar. She went out all guns blazing with a strong brand that got her recognised from the start. She was Ignited from day one - you see I can't help using her own language to describe her - that's how aligned she is!

So let me share with you a little bit about that process because one of the things that really upsets me, as you may well have picked up on by now (!) is people who've got amazing business ideas coming from a real place of passion and purpose, who then don't share what they are doing with any kind of conviction, not being bold and brave with it. I know it's not easy if you are not a big character. I know it can feel scary as f*ck. But it's necessary if you really want to make impact.

So how did Louisa raise the roof with her message? Let's find out…

Louisa:

> "The real key for me was actually the name, and Mamas Ignited came to me after a few sleepless nights when I was trying to make sense of everything. I knew 'what' I wanted to do, and I was totally connected to the 'why' I wanted to do it - what I wasn't sure about was the 'how' I was going to communicate it. I knew it needed real gusto as I literally felt a fire in my belly, so I knew my brand needed to have this energy - and that's where the ignited came from. When I saw the words, **Mamas Ignited** on the page that was it. It was literally born. And from there as a teacher of English and a lover of a metaphor and an analogy I started delving into research to see how I could bring more depth to the name.
>
> I found out that there was a term called the 'bloomery' - a traditional furnace where rock would be smelted to melt the metal - and when the precious metal is extracted from the rock it's called the bloom - this felt very very in tune for what I was setting out to do with my clients - help then break free to bloom! - so the ignite part felt good, and the Mama bit was

*a natural as that's what my daughter Emilie calls me, and my
first thought was to help other mums, who may have lost
themselves a bit too.*

*Next came a total chance finding that brought a further
dimension to my message and brand. Well you might say it
was chance, or you might say it was a guided intervention,
depending on how 'woo' you are! - but I found this quotation
when scrolling one day that literally leapt out at me. I had
just started my business and I saw this meme on Facebook. It
said 'An ironing board is a surfboard that gave up on its
dreams' and I thought 'My God - yes!' I'm the ironing
board."*

I remember Louisa sharing this with me as we were working
with her at this point to help her bring her brand to life and I
literally got goosebumps. It got a huge YES from me in terms
of being a message she could really stand behind and bang her
drum about. THIS would get her noticed. THIS would make
people sit up and SEE her and this made SENSE - because it
100% totally and utterly connected to her story. She indeed
had been the ironing board and she was now igniting others to
get on their surfboard instead.

Louisa:

> *"I'd been stuck behind my teaching ironing board for 16 years. I realised I needed to turn it back into a surfboard. I needed to find my fire, to ignite myself to go and surf. It was just wonderful to feel this really come together. I invested in getting my branding done by JoJo Smith at CreativSAS and it all just fell into place. It was super strong. I remember I put the meme on Facebook and at this point I didn't really have a following but the number of comments I got from people was amazing. And so that was it. I was **Mamas Ignited** - and the more I do, the more this brand becomes me - the more I ignite and the more I step into my power, the stronger it becomes."*

This is the sign of a powerful brand, one that grows with you and just gets better and better as you evolve. Working from core foundations provides such an incredible grounding, and it provides a really strong base to grow from and when you have gusto with your messaging too then you hit the jackpot. When your audience 'gets you' from day one - when they quickly understand what you're all about you're nailing it - when they love it and want to be a part of it you're laughing!

Throughout Louisa's journey we've worked with her to help her position her brand messaging, to connect her story to her business and to make her mission easy to understand. She brought the fire (you see I'm doing it again, I can't help it!) from day one. She has followed our advice to the letter, and she is a living breathing example of PR gold.

For her first branding shoot we made sure we were playful with her image and a 50's inspired style, (which was one she already embraced naturally anyway) incorporating the house-wife look and the ironing board brought kick ass visual assets into the mix too.

Louisa let us introduce her to national media from launch. There was no hanging around here and there was no need for it - we were press ready, we were prepared, we were strong in the identity we were introducing to the press. We've shared her story on the radio, on podcasts, in women's magazines, in entrepreneurial titles and even celebrated her being featured in Forbes (now THAT was a day of high-pitched squeals!!) She's been approached for speaking gigs, has been shortlisted in awards and has opened doors to collaborations and partner-ships that are set to see her business boom....all in less than twelve months, because she committed to really bringing her brand to life from the start.

Because she was brave. Because she was bold. Because she stood strongly behind her message.

Louisa:

> *"I have to admit it was really really well-planned and thought through, because I knew that I wasn't playing and I invested in getting the best team on my side from the start. With Chocolate PR, CreativSAS and Dani Wallace all in my corner how could I fail?*

> *But I just also want to add here that even though I went all in*

and embraced being bold and strong with my brand it doesn't mean it was all easy. You've got to really commit to it and trust yourself as well. Nobody else can have your ideas. You know, you're selling yourself in your unique personality at the end of the day, and that's what your USP is in your business.

*And it's funny because you hear so much speak of imposter syndrome and limiting beliefs, which I have, and I now have level-up imposter syndrome, but back then, it was almost like I was devoid of that because I was just so intent on this mission - like nothing could stop me. I just went all in and before I knew it, I was the ironing board lady. People recognised me. The colours of my branding were recognisable and it all came together and it's just grown and grown within that strong **Mamas Ignited** identity. So many people tell me 'you ignite me' 'you've ignited me'. I'm blown away by this."*

It's no surprise to me that she has people speaking her language back to her. It's not surprising that I do it. It comes down to the fact she is so consistent in her message and in her being a queen at rinse and repeating. This is one of the fundamental things we teach our clients to do - to OWN their 'thing' and Louisa has done this over and over again in a really, really strong way. When you do this you get rewarded because people recognise you for that.

So the lingering message I want to leave you with from Louisa's fabulous success story is - to turn up the dial! Whatever you're doing, turn up the frickin' dial, turn it up so that people can not, not know what you stand for. People need to see you everywhere and see that visual representation as well. Get ignited!

Connect...

Connect with Louisa and Mamas Ignited via

https://www.instagram.com/mamasignited/ and

https://www.facebook.com/mamasignited and

https://mamasignited.co.uk/

7

AGADOO

"*Ag-a-doo-doo-doo,* push pineapple, shake the tree *Aga-doo-doo-doo,* push pineapple, grind coffee."

— CREDITS: BLACK LACE 1984

Do you remember this song from your childhood? Do you remember enthusiastically jumping around at school discos or holiday clubs trying your darndest to get all the actions right (whilst if you were anything like me, getting them all hopelessly out of time?!)

Or what about the one where you had to be Superman...

"*Jump, swim, spray, ski and Supermaaaaaaan.*"

— CREDITS: BLACKLACE 1983

These always seemed like so much fun didn't they, and we were really proud when we knew all the actions! Take this a little further into adulthood and perhaps at the Uni student bar you had a bit of the Macarena or Saturday Night Wigfield action... or what's that one where you sit on the floor all in a line and sway to the left and right, forwards and backwards? I have no idea of it's name, but it was a favourite of mine! - oh memories, memories!

I was ALL over these dances, totally loved them and the feeling of being a part of something as a group, of feeling a sense of togetherness, of laughing and joking as we all looked like equal idiots.

Let me ask you - how often these days do you try and do a bit of Agadoo? How often do you try and follow suit, to copy the moves of what others are doing, and stay in time with them? I wonder how aware you are of it you do this or not? I'll be honest - this has been a massive downfall of mine, especially since entering the online space.

You see I haven't been in this world for that long. My business was built in the 'traditional world' of having a bricks and mortar office for over ten years, having an in-person team, going to local networking events, running PR for companies based within our region, going to their offices for meetings, going out for lunches etc. Here I had found my feet, here I was confident of my brand character after having worked out how to use my qualities to stand out. Often in the minority in a room full of men in suits, I was the short feisty fun blonde PR girl who disrupted the boring networking breakfasts with her cheeky sense of humour, leather skirts and stories of having been out entertaining clients until 4am (a few hours earlier!) I quickly worked out that by bringing the real me to the party I attracted clients I loved to work with and repelled those I didn't suit. It worked a treat. We had some incredible clients, fun and creative, disrupters of their industries, making waves and growing really recognisable brands.

As the business grew, we started to attract bigger and bigger brands - I'm talking Yo! Sushi, Whistles, Marriott Hotels, and organisations like 150 year old training companies and 100 year old Building Societies. What we could do with these clients expanded, and the brand I had built up with Chocolate PR of offering *'tasty creative solutions'* was in demand. These big brands loved us as a boutique agency, fuelled by creative ideas and we started to gain access to the kind of budgets that enabled us to run incredible events and develop multiple award-winning campaigns for these clients. I loved this work for many years and we really had built up a strong identity.

But, as with anything you have done for over ten years the novelty started to wear off and as we had risen to work with bigger companies, the joy also started to diminish. The realities of having to spend hours in boardrooms, often with thirty people - maybe two of whom understood or gave a shit about PR was draining. The battles of having to fight for your ideas (that they were paying you for) when they had *'always done it this way'* became exhausting. They wanted to do the Superman dance repeating all the same moves, but we were trying to get them to create their own moves and were often met with a lot of resistance at the higher levels.

Couple this increasing stress and diminishing lack of satisfaction with a personal life of having a young child which only gave me 4 hours sleep a night, and then a run of really shitting personal life traumas. These included my husband getting run over and breaking his back - only narrowing avoiding being paralysed, a missed miscarriage which floored me and triggered old trauma, and threatening abusive neighbours causing stress at home. I hit breaking point. I had no energy left to play the game in the corporate world, to jump to the left, or to the right... I had no energy for it nor had I any desire to do it. I decided my time and my energy was too precious to be playing *Agadoo* with marketing managers with their own agendas... we were not dancing in time, and it was all getting too awkward.

So I walked away.

Have you done this?

Did you feel like this in corporate? Did you say, *'no more'*? Have you taken control of your life and career direction? It can feel empowering, stepping off the treadmill you somehow found yourself on and moving in a new direction? But it's also scary as fu*k because then who are you? Where do you fit in? What credibility do you have when you go in a new direction?

When I decided to move away from the corporate space I went all in for change. I gave up the office, I reduced the size of the team, I reduced my working hours - all in a very knee jerk reaction way to getting rid of what was making me stressed... but then what? I didn't want to quit PR - I just wanted to find a new purpose and focus for my skills... and I wanted to have some fun again!

Enter the world of female entrepreneurship and female focused networking groups. I was invited to attend a local in person networking event for women who had quit their corporate worlds to start up new businesses, along with women who were aiming to quit their 9-5. These women didn't do Agadoo. They made up their own dances and Oh My God, I loved them for that!

Because when you've been conditioned for so long you rebel right? Well you do if you're anything like me! I connected with these women, I was energised by them, I was inspired by them, and I wanted to help them. I wanted them to embrace their individuality and unique offers they had to share with the world (which ironically they didn't truly see, value or appreciate) and so it began - my work to empower these women and others like them, to dance their own dance - and bloody well celebrate it.

Consider here when you have played Agadoo? Perhaps when you've created your business name - does is sound like everyone else's? When you've created a Facebook group or a course - would people instantly be able to say that is 100% you or could it be anyone's? When you've written Top Ten tips on your blog or in a social post? Does it SCREAM your character, or could your competitors have written it?

The first step to being able to stand out more is self-awareness of what you are currently doing. When I first joined the online space, I was definitely trying to fit in rather than stand out, thanks to that good old imposter syndrome - but all this does is waste time. It stops you being magnetic, it makes you blend into the rest of the noise.

To really lead your space, to really make an impact you must be brave. You must be bold. You must dare to be seen, like Louisa (who I introduced you to in the last chapter). She didn't join in with Agadoo - she stood proudly with her unique identity and this is what led to her creating an impactful business which is changing lives....just like Dani Wallace and her *I am The Queen Bee Movement*.

This is a lesson I want you to fast track, one I want you to grab hold of because when you stop doing Agadoo and start doing you - that's when the magic truly happens!

⚡ Activity....

What more of you do YOU need to bring to the party? Where
could you zig where other zag?

Make a note here!

Energy

Innovation

Caring.

Get shit done attitude.

Premium ~ high level.

Sophistication

Gravitas ~ charisma.

Uath

8

YOUR FIRST MOVE

It's decision time. You've seen the power of PR and are ready to stand up and be counted, now it's time to make a move in getting your PR party started.

So, what's your first move going to be?

Where do you start?

When playing the PR game YOU need to make the first move. Remember you have to be the party planner not the one who waits around for the invite. You need to be the one that takes control, because sitting around and hoping a journalist picks up the phone to call you is only going to lead to misery! You've got to create your own opportunities, but you're not starting from ground zero.

The good news is that opportunities are ready and waiting for you!

Here are 5 ways you can get your PR party started:-

1. Launch PR
2. Real Life Story PR
3. Profile PR/Interviews
4. Expert/ Knowledge Sharing PR
5. Topical PR

Let's take these one at a time so you can see which one is going to be THE one for you. You can do all of these, eventually you will, but you've got to start somewhere, and that's what we're looking for, your way in, your foot in the door....

1. Launch PR

Let's start at the very beginning. If you haven't yet launched your business via PR this is a no brainer. This one gets me really giddy because it's such an easy one - but one that sooooooo many entrepreneurs miss out on - so sharing this with you feels like my duty and seeing you celebrate your business in the press will make me super happy! Please do share your wins and tag me and I will share with our audience too! This one is also an easy one as the best place to start is with local media (more on that in the next chapter).

If you haven't yet told your story of why you have started your business this is for you. Your launch story is a PR gift.

If you think back to all the things we know the media want - human interest, real people, stories that inspire and motivate, and for local PR celebration and showcasing of local people who have 'done good' - then you already know that you're onto a winner as your launch story PR is ticking ALL the boxes.

The other thing we need to remember is the rule of storytelling and not selling - because with launch PR it can be so tempting to forget this rule in the excitement of telling the world about your new business but don't block yourself from success. You can still share information about your business but keep it mission focused and informative rather than sales focused in tone.

Let's remember WHAT you need to communicate - what we want to know is what's behind your business, what's the story of your business. I know you're driven by your passion and purpose, and have quite likely left the corporate rat race to do something you truly love so let's inspire others with this story.

Your launch PR story should share your journey of how you've come to be here, doing what you're doing. It should share your defining moment that made you make the decision to start your business and it also needs to reference the path you took along the way. It needs to share YOU, so readers can connect with you on a very human level and find resonance with your journey. This is the part many people struggle with, as it can feel strange to start sharing your inner thoughts, and vulnerabilities and personal reasons why you have made the decisions you have. When working in corporate this is not the done thing. In day-to-day life we are told to keep our personal life to ourselves, to just get on with things and sharing our inner thoughts is not something that will particularly come naturally to us.

But this is the backbone of PR and also a key element of marketing in the online space, because where we can't meet people in real life and connect with them through chats over wine or sharing a cuppa we need to fast track the process of building relationships, and sharing information about you and your journey is a key way of doing this.

Being prepared to share openly and honestly your ups and downs, your learnings, and your discoveries about yourself really is important to building relationships online and making this kind of PR work.

Think about your business and what you're doing then ask yourself:

- Why are you so driven to do this?
- What life circumstances have led you to have this mission and focus?
- What part of your journey to get here are you happy to share?
- What is your mission for your business? - What's your bigger purpose? Think further than just the products and services you sell and think about the wider impact that you want to make.
- Why is your business needed. Consider if there is a gap in the market - if there are any stats to show why what you do is needed that's even better - there quite probably will be.

Also don't forget to use the credibility of your corporate life, much as you may have hated it. Think about using it for good, as a way to showcase that you can be trusted. I know you don't necessarily feel validated by your corporate success, but it definitely helps build credibility in the eyes of journalists. When we have introduced clients using titles such as *'ex Marketing Manager of HSBC'*, *'Learning & Development Training Manager at Virgin'* you can see the media stand up and take more notice than when we don't have these titles to throw in. I know it shouldn't make a difference, but it does, so if you have these titles to use I encourage you to do so - you might as well make the most of those years (which you quite probably have negative associations with) - make them work for you!

The route to launch PR is usually via a press release as this is the way you can provide your story on a plate, so they can just lift it into their publication. A press release is written in the 3rd person as if it has come from an interview so you really are doing the hard work for the journalist, so they can copy and paste the info. *[See the resources link at the end of the chapter to access a launch press release template]*

The other thing that's super important with launch PR - indeed all PR - is imagery. Get prepared. Get PR ready. Make sure you have good strong high-resolution images that help tell the story of your business. You don't necessarily need a professional photographer, (although it also helps to boost your own confidence when you take this step) but you do need a professional approach. Make sure you have a clear background, nothing too fussy, you have a focus on what you're trying to say with your image, and present the media with a mixture of photos that support your story.

All sounds do-able right? Will you promise me that if you haven't yet launched your business via PR you will? PLEASE!!!! It's such an opportunity there for the taking, yet so many people miss out on this PR Gold - don't be one of them! And remember here you don't need to be in pre-launch for this to work. If you've been in business for up to a year and not yet shared the launch of it via the media this is still there to do. If it's longer than that you will need a timely hook to tell it - such as a business growth story if you are employing people, or a celebration of hitting a certain level in business, or winning an award - all of these can be reasons to go to the media, to share your timely news, and then you weave in your backstory to make the story deeper.

2. Real Life Stories

If you've managed to get on board with the idea of sharing your story and braving it to remove the mask and reveal the real you then you might as well go bigger than just local media with it. There are plenty of opportunities to also share your story with national media and women's mags (more on who to target in the next chapter).

So, what do you need to know about this kind of PR? It needs to totally lead from the heart and the business element will definitely be secondary here. Think about what these types of pieces look like - think about when you read these articles in women's weeklies what is it that draws you in?

It's the headline right? Or the imagery? So be aware that for real life stories the media love the drama. This can be hard to accept as I know your story cannot be summed up in one cheesy dramatic clickbait headline and indeed we do not want to necessarily focus on all the negatives which are usually what the headlines includes, but think of it like this....you have to play the game.

To get into the party, past the bouncers, you have to show you are the right fit for them - and this means giving them what they need. If they need the drama for the headline just try and accept this based on the fact that that will bring more readers to your article - it will draw more people in so you can support more people with your work. You know you are not defined by a headline so don't let it be a big deal. Be prepared to be uncomfortable and for the fact that when you see your article in print you may feel very vulnerable....but use this, share your thoughts and feelings with your audience as you share your PR wins on social media and I guarantee your audience will show support and love.

3. Profile PR Opportunities

If you are not comfortable in sharing your whole story but would like to help people get to know you a bit more then profile interviews can be nice middle ground. These articles are usually based around a set of questions, like an interview, and you have the chance to share as much or as little as you'd like around each area. Usually covering who you are and what you do now, as well as your journey to getting here there is a chance to make sense of why you are doing what you're doing but it's lighter touch than a full real-life story. Usually there are also very specific questions around your business in these so you can be a bit more direct about your services.

4. Expert PR

If sharing your story is something you're not ready for, or if you'd like to be recognised as an expert in your space, then knowledge sharing via PR is the right first move for you.

This approach requires a lot less of your story - although it still needs a nod to it - you don't get away with not giving ANY of you - but it could be a paragraph intro that wraps it up in a nutshell, just to set the scene as to why you are the right person to offer advice and guidance on this subject area.

In these kind of introductions we encourage you to sum up your story in a nutshell via this format - *"I am….and I…..so that ….. because………"* as this helps journalists see why you should be trusted as an expert, and also why you care about your subject matter.

The *'I am'* should be used to qualify and describe you - introduce yourself in the best possible light - e.g. I am award winning, I am an ICF accredited coach, I am a nutritionist with over twenty years' experience specialising in food intolerances, I am a best-selling author, I am a global speaker… etc.

'and I' is a straight, direct statement about what you do - *help high achieving women to find calm in their busy rial lives'*, or *'I help women struggling with anxiety to*

tap into tools that support them to feel less stressed and more in control'… etc.

The **'so that'** is where you talk about the impact you make with your work, the effect you have on the lives of your clients. For example *'so that they can enjoy life rather than struggle through life'*, or *'so that they can feel more empowered and less a victim of their struggles'*…etc.

The **'because'** bit is where you nod to your story and show you have been there, that you have empathy for others in your old shoes – *'because I know how it feels to be the one falling apart in silence and how this can ruin your relationships and lead to spiralling despair'*, or *'because I am on a mission to change the industry that is leading people down the wrong path and creating a nation of people with unhealthy relationships with food'*, or *'because having tried to take my own life several times after feeling like I had no other choice, I want to show people that there are other paths even in the depths of despair and I'm here to support them.'*

Once you have introduced yourself in this way you have ticked the boxes of illustrating to the journalist why you should be given a voice, the next thing to decide is what you want to have a voice on.

What knowledge are you here to share? What message are you so passionate about communicating, what does your audience need to know from you?

As with the real-life story stuff the headline again is key, but this time rather than drama you're looking for communicating the power of your message around your subject area. Using surprising or challenging headlines that make people stop and think, using words that you don't necessarily expect to go together, or questions that raise an eyebrow are great ways of engaging people and drawing them in.

In terms of your content keep it simple - go with five to a maximum of ten top tips around one core subject area, with a bit of an introduction to set the scene. Don't try to share all you know - you will just overwhelm and confuse people. See it as an opportunity to introduce them into your world. They will learn from you, take something actionable from you, and therefore as a result start to value and trust you.

Also, ideally at this point you have a freebie to point them towards, so you're bringing people into your world more permanently. Offer a free guide or download and make this sit behind a page that captures their email so you can get them on your list and nurture them. PR can be a real driver for building your audience when used this way

5. Reactive & Topical PR

All of the above require proactive pitching to a journalist - this can be referred to as *Proactive PR*, and can take time to get your head around and effort to prepare the content. If you're looking for a quick win with your first PR move, then *Reactive PR* could be a good way to go as it's fast and potentially a way to nail your first big media trust tag.

Reactive PR is when you respond to a journalist enquiry, so you're helping them out in their time of need. You're being their resource, their expert, their case study. Often these requests are timely or related to topical content or news agendas, so deadlines are tight and turnarounds are fast but in many cases these opportunities create great results as when you don't have time to faff you get straight to the point and this hits the mark! We've had clients featured in Forbes and Newsweek and many many other national media as a result of *Reactive PR.*

National media use this as part of their everyday practices so you can get into some really big titles via this route. We support clients a lot with this form of PR, feeding PR opportunities to them whether that's 121 or via our membership to help them capitalise on what's available, but you can also tap into some of these opportunities for yourself via the power of *Twitter*. Searching the hashtag #journorequest or #casestudyrequest can open many doors. If you've never tried this I'd encourage you to take a look, even if you're not ready to take action yet, just so that you can see what's out there, and also so you can get familiar with key journalists in your area of specialism and they start to feel more familiar to you - this makes them more human and less scary and can make a huge difference around how you feel when approaching them.

More coming in the next chapter around 'how' to do this, so fret not! For now, I just want you to consider which of the above routes feels best to you.

———

⚡ **Activity....**

What's your first move going to be? Which route to the PR party feels the right one to start with?

⚡ **HELP...**

Find Press Release templates and examples of media coverage of all the different types mentioned at https://chocolatepr.co.uk/celebrating-you-with-pr/resources

↳ Launch PR
 Profile PR
 Expert PR.

9

INVITING YOUR GUESTS

W e've now considered your first move - and that's pretty exciting - but who are you going to bring along for the ride? As we all know a party is no good without guests... although I know the introverts amongst you might disagree! Often this is the part we stress about the most - who do we invite? We must make sure we choose the right people. What if they don't come? What if NO-ONE comes and we get totally and utterly rejected? That would suck big time right? That would be enough to make us never want to plan a party ever again!

Now we are going to deal with the process of inviting guests - aka journos- to your celebration party.

We know from our lovely clients at *Chocolate PR* that often this is the bit that holds people back - it's the pitching bit that they see as scary. You build up the journalists in your mind, giving them this huge gravitas, and seeing them as having this real power over your success or failure.

We often compare the feeling of phoning up a journalist for the first time to making that call as a young teenager of the 70s/80s, to your wannabe boyfriend or girlfriend at the time. You had to build yourself up to making that call - an actual phone call (as there was no other tech at the time!) - your heart is beating, you are sweating, you hang up ten times before you actually see the call through... you rehearse what you're going to say a million times in your head first, you feel terrified of what they might say when you put yourself out there. Will they think you are an idiot? Will they laugh at you? Will they hang up on you? These are the thoughts we play out before we play out the alternative options of it actually going our way!

This is how many people build up their first interaction with press - and this used to be the only way pitching was done. We'd have to make the calls, get maybe 30-60 seconds to get what we had to say out before we got stopped in our tracks, hoping we'd manage to attract interest within that timescale of their tiny attention span!

These days it is unlikely that your first interaction with a journalist will be by phone. Email is your friend that saves you from this quite brutal process - but I know even via the online route many people do experience the same kind of fear.

Journalists don't have the best rep - often painted as intimidating or not to be trusted in TV and films - we have this image that they are sat in an ivory tower just waiting for us to dare to press send on the email - then they kick back in their chair laughing their heads off shouting *"WHO does this person think they are, sending me an email? WHY would I want to run their story? You've got to be kidding me!"* DELETE!

But obviously this isn't the case (most of the time!) and we need try and get some of your power back.

I always try to remind our clients that just like us, they're human and they don't bite! At a recent event where I hosted a media panel, the lovely Anna Jameson, a reporter, and presenter at BBC Manchester touched on how often our stereotypical idea of a journalist can be intimidating, especially if it is your first encounter with the media. I think what she said is worth sharing:

> *Journalists are just like you. Everyone has their own insecurities; everyone has their own anxieties and we just want do our best as well. We are here to share your stories - we need them and want to hear them - so never ever be afraid of approaching the media."*

This is our experience too - on the whole journos are open and receptive to hearing from you… if you play by the rules.

Ok - so what rules? How can you play by the rules if you don't know what they are? And here lies the problem. Most people who pitch to the press have no idea what they are doing - they have had no guidance and just charge in full steam ahead hoping for the best. This is usually when it goes wrong as you do rile them. You do play into the things they hate about being pitched to - if you've not done the hard work first, so let's get you ready.

STEP 1: Understanding What They Need

Firstly, it's important when you're pitching to the media, to gauge an understanding of what the media landscape looks like. Since the move to more digital publications and the decrease of print news, much of the news people read is online and this cycle never stops. So, if one thing is for certain it's that journalists are busy and they don't have much time. Be aware of this. Respect this.

This is where refining your story and content comes in. You do this by doing the prep work for them and presenting the info you'd like them to share on a plate - with sprinkles on top - helps to make the exchange between yourself and the journalist much easier and for them to know if your story/content is the right fit for them. It shows you are press ready.

What do they need when you invite them to your party? What do you need to provide on the invite?

- Give them all the info - no-one likes the idea of going to a party when they don't really know what to expect. Too many questions are not good. Mystery is not good. Journalists like details, and lots of them. When you're interacting with journalists, whether that's on the phone, via email, social media or even in person, it's important to be able to get all key info across - in one breath/paragraph. Try to remember and include all the 5 Ws - WHO, WHAT, WHERE,

WHEN, WHY especially when it is a timely story you are pitching.

- Journalists need to know you will throw a good party. No-one has time to waste on shit parties, and in this case journalists don't have time for your party if it doesn't scream out that it's made for them. You need to know how to write for the press - you must write your content in 3rd person - i.e. Helen is celebrating this, not I am celebrating this - so that this can read as if they have already interviewed you. They like it to look like they have done the ground work even if they haven't. Your dream is that they copy and paste what you send them as this means you are in total control of your message and content. The best way to get your head around this is to read read and read some more of the articles in your desired publication - get a feel for their style of article and replicate that.

[*More on this on our press release guide in our resources*]

- Journalists need to be able to visualise what the party will look like and they need to be given the confidence that it will be an experience worth having. Try and add some colour, try to give them an essence of what sort of a person you are and why you're a person worth celebrating or give them a flavour of what you're bringing to the party. You can do this with your language but also one of the biggest ways to attract attention in the media is through impactful imagery. Journalists are always competing to get their readers to stop and engage with their content (as opposed to being distracted by other things). They need strong images to go with your story and don't really have the resources these days to provide photographers like they used to - so if you can provide good quality, high-res creative images that really bring your story to life then you get brownie points.

- Journalists need to know what's in the goody bag. When considering if to use your content or not journalists are always thinking what you are leaving their readers with - is there value in this content that will help guide, inspire, motivate, or entertain their readers? If so, then they have hit the jackpot with engagement and that is what makes readers keep coming back. Think about what lasting message you are leaving them with, or if your content is more knowledge sharing then what tips you can provide, what actionable steps could you leave them with, so the reader gets a win from having read your content. Start by looking at the type of things they write about and think if there is anything new you can add to this conversation or what expertise you have that can elevate the work they are already doing. You *can* pitch pure knowledge sharing content - you don't HAVE to use your story as the prime focus - there are lots of ways to get press coverage by sharing what you know - the secret to success here is really targeting who you invite to this party (more on that in a bit!) as it's much more niche and not for everyone.

Those are a few things to be aware of that will help you when it comes to pitching to the press - but I also want you to shift how you think about the balance of power in this relationship.

When you're thinking about pitching your story to a journalist, try and imagine it as more of an exchange. They NEED to be invited to your party, as without parties, they have no publications. They need your content and you need your coverage. Journalists are constantly looking out for new stories, leads and interesting things to write about so your story is not an inconvenience to them but is a way of you helping them out. Try to remember this as it can take the edge off the fear you might feel when putting yourself out there!

STEP 2 - Understanding how they work

Getting under the skin of how something works is another way to remove fear about it. Think about how you take the mystery out of anything new you decide to embark on. As entrepreneurs we've learnt a fair few random skills in our time right? Well, this is no different. To master something, you must first understand the process and the steps involved, as well as having an awareness of how it all plays out.

So with regards to pitching to the press I think it's important you get to know that there are different ways to do it. There are different paths to go down. Specifically, there are two main types of pitching to be aware of.

I referred to this in passing in the last chapter but it's time to dive deeper now as we look set Reactive Pitching and Proactive Pitching.

Let's deal with these one at a time.

The most traditional way of pitching to the media is by proactively inviting them to you party via *Proactive PR*. This, I imagine is the kind of pitching you are aware of - having to reach out to a journalist via email usually, to send them your story, or some content you'd like to share and introduce yourself to them. This is how it's been done for donkeys' years and there is still very much a place for this. This way of working relates back to all of the points above in Step 1.

What else can I tell you about how to make a success of this route?

- **Research is key** - making sure you're putting forward content relevant to them is a biggie - so having researched the publication and pinpointed a section where you've seen similar articles or advice will reap rewards. Letting them know that you see a very specific place for your content helps the journalist believe you're right for them.
- **Make sure your tone suits the publication**. If you have a certain brand character and it's a strong one - you might not be for everyone. Your language absolutely should reflect you and I'm not a fan of dumbing down to fit in, so if you do have a strong style of language it's important to 'find your people' - don't waste your time pitching to media who will never gel with you
- **Don't be vague** - when you're introducing yourself to the media be EXACT about what you're offering

whether that's a story (write it in a press release), or an advice piece (write it as a 5 or 10 top tips piece)

- **Use clear keyword specific subject headers** in your email intros so the journalist can grasp quickly what you're offering and also can find it in future if the time's not right immediately, so that when they need someone on your subject area they can retrieve your email quickly and easily.

It's all comes down to how you can be of service to the journalist. This is true of whatever way you pitch to them.

The other way of pitching is a more recent addition to PR - *Reactive PR*. Since the rise of social media this route is now one journalists love to tap into as a way of them quickly and efficiently reaching out to potential contributors.

Reactive PR and pitching puts the boot on the other foot and this is journalists reaching out to YOU to invite you to THEIR party. This sounds good right?! If they need you surely they are going to be nice, friendly, grateful?

Well yes and no. They are certainly grateful but not always massively friendly as this is a game of speed - there's no time for small talk it's straight into third base!!

Here is an example of how these opportunities can look.

For example this last hour these are some of the journo call outs that have come via this route...

- *Looking for a psychologist/life coach who can comment on sex and relationships for an urgent article for the Express. Please DM/email me at mared.gruffydd@reachplc.com if you can help! Thank you*
- *TWITTER @kateonthinice Are you a woman who has overcome adversity? I would love to share your story on my blog http://dld.bz/hkKgW so please get in touch today. #women #adversity bloggerrequest*
- *EMAIL: Sian.Bradley@metro.co.uk Looking to talk to career experts about what we are really looking for in our jobs/careers post-pandemic, following the news that one in five employees expect to change jobs this year, for metro. Deadline midday. Sian.Bradley@metro.co.uk :)*

You see they are short, direct and to the point - and this is the kind of response they want in return - this is the exact reason they use Twitter as the place to reach out via this route, because of the limited characters. It suits their deadlines, and it cuts out all the crap (as there's literally not enough characters).

Traditionally this approach has been reserved for PR agencies only as journalists liaised with us specifically on content they were searching for and we hooked them up with our clients who ticked the boxes but increasingly media are also reaching out through more mainstream channels now - and callouts like these also appear on Twitter via #journorequest as well as via the subscription services we pay for.

This route sounds easier than Proactive Pitching, right? Well yes, to a degree. It's defo easier from a perspective of it feeling 'lighter' - you don't feel so vulnerable this way around as you

KNOW they are in need of the content they are asking for - BUT it is super competitive and so you need to now know what you're doing to be able stand out.

Here are a few tips if you're going to pitch reactively:-

- **Give them what they are asking for.** Don't waste time introducing yourself and building your kudos and then leave out the bit they actually want. If they have asked a question or asked for your view on something give the answer in a quotable response that they can just lift to include in their article.
- **Respond directly on Twitter**, replying back to their tweet so if they are scanning their profile you are on their radar. We don't always know which route the journo will take in terms of gathering their info - as sometimes they allow emails and also DMS. If these are available defo use them to send more detailed info but always also reply directly on *Twitter* just in case that is the method they choose to use that day - make sure your response on Twitter could be used standalone even if you do send more detail via the other routes.
- **Don't waste time asking for more info** - just go back to them based on their initial question- you will only piss them off and they will ignore you if you can't do this.
- **Use images to stand out** - if you can convey your response in an image this works really well and helps

you stand out on their feed - we have had clients get in Forbes as a result of doing this!

- **Be quick!** They often put these call outs when they are on deadline and need a quote yesterday - if there is no deadline noted assume it is ASAP, so jump in with both feet and get yourself noticed for being helpful and efficient!

A barrier people often put in their own way with Reactive Pitching is that they don't have an active Twitter account - as long as it exists it's fine - journos don't go checking if you've got twenty followers or 2million - they don't care - it's just a channel of communication for them, so please don't let this put you off.

- **See journalist call outs as an opportunity to build a media list**. If you get smart and start to search for #journoorequest using certain keywords to see which journalists are writing about your subject area you can build a really powerful bespoke media list - keep a note of their details, follow them on Twitter and add them to a spreadsheet or Trello board. This way when you have something to proactively pitch you have a list of go-to journos who you know write about your subject area. Even better network with them, share their content and comment on it, so you build up a relationship and your chances of getting featured increase massively too.

STEP 3 - Knowing who to invite

Ok, so you have a bit more awareness now of what you need to do to attract the journalists with your content - so the big question left is WHO to target. Who do you invite to your party?

As I just mentioned above keeping an eye out for who writes about your subject via the #journorequests is a great place to start, as is googling the type of headline you have in mind and seeing where else such articles pop up - you might not have £thousands to buy into a media database but contact details are out there so don't tell yourself they're not.

Often in a printed mag the writers are credited at the front with their full names and often email addresses but if not you can usually guess their email from following the format of any that are given - often this is firstname.surname@publicationti tle.co.uk or sometimes the publishing company if it's a big group. The same goes for newspaper journalists - there will usually be contact details printed somewhere - so it's your job to play detective.

Another tip - when looking for who to target don't go straight in at the top! Don't go for the editor as it is not actually their job to source or write up the stories, they have a much bigger picture role - so the types of people you want to go for are the reporters or editorial assistants who tend to do a lot of the researching work. As a rule of thumb this will serve you well!

Deciding specifically who to target largely depends on WHAT you're pitching. Let's take a couple of examples to explore.

YOUR LAUNCH STORY PR

As we have explored in the last chapter this is PR gold.

This is a story that opens many doors, but the first door I would recommend you knock on is that of your local media. It's always best to invite the most familiar friendly faces to the party first right - it gives you confidence when they say yes.

Local media love celebrating local people - it's kinda a part of their job -It's in their remit. They are there to offer inspiration, motivation, education, to their readers, through sharing stories of local people.

If you are achieving great things as an entrepreneur and you have come from a background that makes that success potentially even more empowering, motivating, inspiring, then that story should be shared with that local media because they will want to get behind you. They will want to share your success story and they will want to celebrate you as one of their own. The local media love 'owning' entrepreneurs who come from their region- it's a pride thing - so roll with it!

Celebrating You is most definitely something they should be doing, but the secret here is in going for the right journo at the local press. For example, often people's first port of call is to send their launch story to the business editor or business reporter - I would advise you against this. Business writers often do fall into the category of journalists with self-importance and they see it as their job - even if only writing for the local rag - to report on the big business news of the day.

Now if your local media is different great. If you see them writing about similar stories to you, then go for it - but sense check first. If all they are writing about is local corporates, they may not value your story - WRONGLY - but still this could be the case, so no point banging your head against a brick wall. You'd probably be better going for a Women's writer or life-style writer or family section writer, who have more opportunity to tell the 'people' stories - sometimes there is actually a people section. Go for these sections rather than the business ones as here is the opportunity to really tell your story - and that's what you want. You don't want a one liner about you launching a business - you want a full page spread about why you launched your business, what led you here, what you mission is and why you give a crap about doing what you're doing having quit your highly successful corporate career.

You need to find a writer who will bring you and your mission to life.

Also don't discount radio - radio is a great PR medium as you get to chat about why you're taking this path and really engage your audience personally. For radio you need to be approaching producers and researchers who work on the programmes that have the chat sections.

When you get published in the local media often this can attract attention of the Nationals - so see if it does the hard work for you here. The Nationals scour and source stories from those regional publications because they want to be seen as inclusive and not covering news from London, even though they are quite London centric. They are briefed to actually cover a much wider geographical region so often they source stories from the regional newspapers that they then take and use in their national publications.

It may be that your story gets picked up and people are knocking on your door asking if they can join the party. If not, once you have it published locally take it to Women's mags who do real life stories - the likes of Woman, Woman's Own, New Magazine, Closer, Pick Me Up who all run transformation stories - but be mindful they will not care too much about your business launch, but it's your journey and your transition they will love.

A KNOWLEDGE SHARING ARTICLE/BLOG

If rather than pitching a story you are instead looking to create PR around knowledge sharing and you have some tips you'd like to get published then you might need to take a different route. It depends on the kind of tips they are as to whether local PR will work for this (for example you will have more luck with lifestyle/wellness-based tips than business focused ones) - and it also depends as to whether you can hook it onto something timely like an awareness day so they have a reason to use it in a timely fashion. This works particularly well for radio and if targeting radio it's the producers of the shows that have a 'chat' or interview section that you need - usually breakfast or drive time.

Your other route to explore is going down the road of more niche publications based on the subject area of your tips. We work with lots of health and wellbeing professionals so for their content obviously we direct this at specific health and wellbeing titles - such as Health & Wellbeing Magazine, Planet Mindful, Happiful, Wellbeing News etc.....but we would also look for an angle into wider business titles too as wellbeing can always be connected to business performance, likewise parenting titles are often targeted as well as broader women's mags - it's about just tweaking the content to suit the title you are targeting.

Google a question or a headline and see which types of media are coming up as having covered that before. Be mindful that they won't run something on repeat that they've recently covered but if it's over 6 months ago, or you can bring a different angle to the discussion then there's an opportunity there.

AN ALTERNATIVE APPROACH

So far we have assumed you will be targeting the media who write directly for the publications you want to be featured in - but now I want you to consider this…

Freelancers are your friend.

Freelance journalists write for a number of different titles and they face many of the same challenges we do in that they too have to pitch their stories to the press, they have to fight their way through to get attention and they have to compete against others fighting for the same space… but here's the thing. This is their JOB.

They are professionals at this and usually people who have gone from the inside out - by that I mean they most likely used to work in-house at some media outlet so they know how it all works. They know how to work the systems AND this is their livelihood. They get paid when they have success placing a story so their incentive is high!

So wouldn't it make sense to get a freelancer or two on your side, so they can pitch your story and then you don't have to... yes you still have to pitch to them, but they are much more open and receptive usually and also more collaborative - so they are prepared to try and find a way to make your story work even if you are not 100% pitch perfect -if they can see a way in they will do what it takes to make it work.

Finding freelance journalists is a bit trickier but *LinkedIn* and *Twitter*, and also *Instagram* are great places to start. They often have in their profile the titles they work for so searching for your ideal publication can sometimes bring them up even if they don't have freelance journalist as a term in its own right on their profile.

AND AN EVEN EASIER WIN!

We love a quick win and these days it is getting easier and easier to get published with the rise of online news sites and blog sites. These are your GODSEND because these are equivalent to your bestie - they can always be relied upon to show up - you KNOW they are going to come to the party - no question, they are your safe bet.

There are many online news and blog sites - some specialise in business, some are subject specific, some are regional, some are global - but the thing that unites them all is that you don't actually have to speak to a journalist - yes that's right - you don't actually have to speak to a journalist.

It's not a free rein to get coverage on any kind of crap - you've still got to play by the rules of submitting good content as it can easily get rejected if you don't write it right but at least it takes out one of the big hurdles many fret about.

Some of these require you to create a profile and become accepted as a contributor, others you can just submit as stand-alone content.

Here are a few for you to explore so you can start to get some names on your PR Party guest list!

These are more suited for knowledge sharing pieces than press releases:

> **Thrive Global** (https://forms.monday.com/forms/ 1ea93ad61b03152282b1a7da8d7aed73?r=use1)

> **Medium** - https://medium.com/new-story

> **Authority** https://medium.com/authority-magazine

> **Entrepreneur.com**

These are great for news pieces - chose which suits depending on if you are wellbeing focused or broader business:

> https://smebusinessnews.co.uk/share-your-news-with-us/

> https://wellbeingnews.co.uk/submit-your-news/

Most local newspapers also have a 'Submit Your News' section on their website - along the lines of https://www.theargus.co.uk/send-us-your-news/ - so look for this as somewhere you could send your launch PR story to.

Getting your PR party started is just a process and it's all about playing the game. Take it a step at a time and play by the rules and you've got this. You totally have.

Is it all feeling a bit more real now I'm hitting you with the practical stuff? There is a commitment needed to have PR success - you've got to make some bold moves to get your party started but it's not a dark art. It's not rocket science. You can do it - and I promise you it's so worth it!

———

Activity....

Make a note of 3 publications you could start to research so you can get to know them well enough to invite them to your party

1.

2.

3.

HELP...

Fast track your process of finding the right journalists and get *Chocolate PR* to compile you a bespoke media list. DM me MEDIA LIST (Instagram/com/jochocpr) We also provide you with live media opportunities in our Get in the Press - Live! Membership - find out more about this here -

https://www.chocolatepr.co.uk/membership-join/

10

NO - I'M NOT COMING!

P R party planning is lots of fun but there comes a time in every party planners' prep when they hit a bump in the road - things don't always go 100% to plan -there's usually something sent to try us! Let's get ready for it - if we're prepared we can overcome it!

In this chapter we're diving straight into the conversation of journo rejection and how to deal with it. *"Why would you do this?"* -you might be screaming? *"You just told us how to invite journalists to our party and now you're telling us they will reject us!"* Well, I'm all for positivity - but what kind of guide would I be if I didn't alert you to the pitfalls too?

The honest truth is that some journalists will say *No,* and many say nothing at all - so you need to be ready - but you're not going to be beaten. You're going to take all feedback on the chin and use it in a positive way. Do not worry.

When starting out on your PR journey and you start inviting people to join your PR Party you won't get everyone to say, *"Yes please I can't wait to come...."* And I'm tackling this now as I don't want any negativity to start to eat in if you're not necessarily getting the results that you want straight away.

I am going to arm you with ammunition to deal with this, so if you get a few *No's* in amongst your *Yes's* you're not reduced to a crumpled mess on the floor starting to doubt the need for your very existence.

I am giving you five things to remember when you get a *'No thank you'* from a journalist.

But first let's start by remembering that you're playing a game. What I've been teaching you in the past few chapters are some of the behind-the-scenes ways that you can play the PR game, sharing ways that you can increase your chances of success when you're trying to get yourself free editorial coverage, which is as we know, an absolute privilege.

If you're playing a game, you're playing it with someone else, and when you play a game you're not always going to win. You can learn how to increase your chances of winning. You can learn lots of ways to improve your odds. But ultimately, you're not always going to win and not always going to get a *Yes*. I want you to be able to deal with that. I want you to be able to realise that this is not failure. It doesn't mean that you're no good. It doesn't mean that it's a complete disaster. I want you to know that even with twenty years experience myself and my team get a lot of *No's* - we get a lot of *No's* every day. It's a part of the process.

As with anything *No's* are a part of the path to getting those incredible, incredible celebration yeses.

Here are five things to remember:-

1. It's not personal

This is a really big important one. Often by the time you pitch yourself to a journalist you have already built them up in your mind to be some kind of God, and so when they don't accept your pitch you feel like it's a personal rejection from someone you've built up to be better than you.

A really interesting analogy came out in our challenge recently where one of the ladies said they felt a journalist was part of the popular gang, like at school - and that they weren't in the same gang. They explained how they wanted to be in the gang but felt like the underdog, an outsider. This was one of the reasons they were nervous about approaching journalists because of this kind of image that they had of them - does that resonate with you?

When we build somebody up like this it's hard to be rejected by them - but what we need to remember is it's not rejection. If you have pitched something to a journalist or if you have responded to a request that they've put out and you either haven't heard back or you've had a very polite *'no thank you not this time'*, please take it for what it is. It simply means that it's not quite right for them at this second, and there's lots and lots of reasons for that.

It might be that they've already found someone they wanted well before the deadline, and they don't need anything at that particular moment. It might be that they already have an existing relationship with someone else who can talk about that subject matter, and they've gone with them this time. It might be they had a completely different agenda in mind, so you just weren't the right fit. And it might be that the angle they were after was something unspoken, that they didn't even communicate properly, so you were never going to be able to hit the mark anyway. It could be any of these things.

Likewise, if you've pitched something proactively to them, rather than responding to a request, and they say *No*, it could just mean they haven't quite understood what you're about. They might not have got all the detail of how you could fit in with what you've suggested. Another level of information may be required. It could be that it's too early in your relationship with them for that to have landed at that point - if it's not something that they are desperate to write about, then it can take a little bit longer. Please remember it's not personal, and use the process to build resilience. Resilience is so important in PR it really, really is because it's not a one hit wonder. It's not something that just happens as if by magic. You send out your ideal PR piece and it gets picked up in the national media the next day... party time yes... But very, very rarely does that happen.

PR is a process and it's something that we have to commit to doing on a long-term basis.

2. You won't get blacklisted

Many people are fearful of sending things to the media because they fear if they get it wrong and send the wrong information, or they don't send the stuff that the journalist uses straight away then it's the end of the road for them. You think you'll get blacklisted. You believe the journalist hates you and you will never ever get PR ever in your entire life. That isn't how it works. Largely because of the pace of journalism and their need for consistent current content means they're always looking. They don't cross people off their lists unless you've sent them something really, really terrible, which you will not have done. If you've followed all of our steps you won't be blacklisted. So please don't think that by sending something that doesn't hit the mark the first time that that's the end of the road for you. I don't want you to put that much pressure on yourself. I want to remove that pressure and for you to realise that a no is just a not right now. You will not get blacklisted. They won't ignore you the next time you tweet. So please don't create more out of this interaction than there is - because they certainly don't.

3. Remember your content isn't crap - but check how you're communicating it

I realise this might be quite a hard thing to grasp if you've been knocked back a few times by journalists, if you've been putting content out there and it's not hitting, it's not biting. There are a few things that you can do to sense check the content you're sending.

I'm going to deal with this one based on it being a reactive enquiry you're responding to (i.e. a journo request or a media alert we have sent you) because when you commit to PR and you start to get in the flow of responding to things like this and you don't hear anything back this *can* feel rather soul destroying.

So, let's look into what goes on here.

If the opportunity has come in thick and fast and it's on deadline the natural thing to do is to rattle your response off. You don't want to miss out so best get something over to them sharpish. Well, yes and sometimes this does work to your advantage (if it's totally your topic and you could reply in your sleep). Sometimes your gut wins through with killer content that cuts through the rest and the response you've knocked up in five mins in between making the kids tea and walking the dog is the one that gets you published. But more often than not rushing a response means you might be forgetting a few key things and you could improve the way you responded to increase your chances of inclusion. Remember we're trying to give journalists as many reasons as possible to say *Yes*, not reasons to say *No*.

A quick checklist when responding to reactive media requests:-

1. Really look at what they've asked for and challenge yourself to see if you've answered their question fully. It's easy to get so wrapped up the point YOU want to make that you've not answered the point the journo

was trying to get to. Answer their question. Answer it simply and quickly, in as few characters as possible (you can always add more info but it's ideal for them if they can lift a tweet or a one or two liner to copy and paste into their piece)

2. Is there an opportunity to provide a photo? Do you have one that supports your point? If so send -having interesting scroll stopping visuals gives you power.

3. Have you given them anything different? If you're replying with the same generic thing as everyone else that is going to lead to failure, go a level deeper or down a different track. If you've submitted responses and it's not working for you be honest with yourself and review if your comment is stand out enough to be used to illustrate their point. You need to make them look good. Are you giving them enough to do this?

4. Have you made it clear you're the perfect person for that response? Have you approached them with conviction and confidence that you're the expert in this, or that your story is so perfect for what they've asked for - confidence is key here! Have you given them a one line bio to use to describe who are and what you do/your credentials as this makes it easier for them too? Have you given them reason after reason to choose you, to trust you, to believe in you to make them feel that you're credible? Sense check whether what you're putting out is the best version of you to really optimise your chances of success.

5. When you get a knock back or get ignored for a piece don't stop there. Go and hunt down the finished

article so you can see what angles they did go with. Google the journo name, publication and some title keywords based on their callout, and you'll be able to find the piece. Don't forget, some don't come out for months whereas some are next day turnaround - the request details will usually give you a bit of a clue on this.

If you've not hit the nail on the head, it's important to learn from these situations and be really honest with yourself. Sometimes if you're honest you will see that you could have put more effort into your reply, more heart and soul in there. You might reflect that you could thought more deeply about that response and written something more specific for them. You live and learn and do better next time.

4. *No* is a step closer to a *Yes*

If you've ever done any sales training in your life, you will have heard this phrase many many times. It comes from the fact that it's often a numbers game when it comes to selling and this is exactly the same when you're trying to target journalists, you're effectively trying to pitch to a group of people. As with the sales process, in PR it works the same - *No* is a step closer to a *Yes* because it means you're on the journey. It means that you're progressing. It means that you're ready to be in these conversations. *A No* is much better than not having tried at all and *No* is getting you in their world and *No* is getting you started in building relationships.

If you've been in a conversation with a journalist, if you have responded to something and it hasn't led to anything, it doesn't have to be the end. It doesn't have to be the end of that conversation. Think about it as an open door. Think about it as a way that you have already entered that world, and now you can go down a different path. Think about if you've engaged with them on *Twitter*, how can you build that relationship on *Twitter*, follow them share their content and comment on their content before you pitch them again. Start to build the relationship up a little bit more before you then do your next pitch because that makes a huge amount of difference if they actually know and connect with you as an individual. It makes a massive amount of difference because you're then not cold pitching. Get involved on Twitter - chat, get involved in some interaction and really get into their world.

Also save their contact details because the people that are reaching out and the ones that you have chosen to respond to are obviously the right journalists for your subject area because otherwise you wouldn't have bothered in the first place. Build up your media database by making these connections and saving their details - make sure that you're not missing an opportunity by crossing them off with a *'oh, well that didn't work'* shrug. Save the contact details and think about how you can retarget, how you can connect with them and use those details for future success because you're going to get future success. You're not doing all of this just have doors banged in your face. No way. You're going to get future success if you're doing it right, so the No's are just a part of the process. They're just a part of the journey and I want you to disassociate from them and stop putting so much emotional connection to them.

5. Retarget and go again

Get back on that horse because we don't want to give up. You don't want to not take these amazing opportunities that are right at your fingertips. So, you've got to go again. And that's where doing this more and more builds up your resistance and your resilience and also you do really start to get a feel for what's working and what isn't working and then you can tweak and adapt your approach.

When you're going to retarget and go again, to give yourself a confidence boost why don't you target someone you know is pretty much a no brainer. Go for someone so specific to your content area, so perfect for your mission and your message and maybe go back down a few levels. So, if you've been pitching quite high end magazines or really big nationals, take it back down to a blog or to an online publication. Take it back down to a publication that you can contribute to online or take it to something that you know you're going to have a success with. Build that confidence back up, share your wins, celebrate those wins, and then go again. Because we are not taking rejection as a failure. You're not taking it as something that means your PR journey is coming to an end before it's even started. We don't take *No* for an answer.

When we are talking to journalists, we don't accept those *No's* we just politely nod and go, '*Okay, that's fine- It's not right this second, what's our next plan of attack?*' How are we going to get in here because we absolutely need to get in here - and then it's all about the research and about the retargeting. It's all about finding those different ways in building those relationships more.

No is not a *No* in our world and I don't want it to be one in yours either. When you commit to spreading your message really believe in it and its power. When you do connect with your PR approach in this way you will get more than just a one hit wonder. This is when you really buy into the power of PR and start to understand the need for consistent pitching, proactive pitching and purposeful pitching, rinsing and repeating your core message. When you recognise this approach is the route to success that's when you're going to reap the rewards, so that's what I want for you - to keep focused, to stay in your own lane and not to get knocked off track if it doesn't quite go to plan on day one.

Is that a deal? Because there's no time for *'It's my party and I'll cry if I want to'* when there's a powerful mission to be spread!

———

HELP...

If at any point you'd benefit from having this message hammered home again get me in your ears via this short podcast episode which talks all about journo rejection -

https://podcasts.apple.com/gb/podcast/pr-powerhouse-with-jo-swann/id1585138279?i=1000537436387

11

GETTING READY TO GO OUT

I'm writing this chapter listening to Apple Music's best of the 80's playlist - oooo there are some belters in here if you ever need a bit of lifting up on a down day! Isn't it amazing how the energy of music can completely change your mood? I'd encourage you to tap into this if you're ever having a wobble in your PR journey as dancing around to an upbeat tune or running like a maniac around the park to it has changed my mindset many a time over and helped me believe I can do anything I set my mind to as I get lost in the power ballad lyrics! It really does work EVERY single time.

This chapter is all about prep - and yes some of this is mental prep that's needed.

We're agreed you're still up for your PR party? You're not letting journo rejection fears get in your way? Didn't think so.

Are there any other little niggles we need to get rid of as you get ready to *step out?*' Are there questions lurking that still need to be answered before you're dancing out the door with your sparkly dress on to your very own PR party?

Preparing for PR activity is very much like preparing for a night out. The more time you have to get ready and the more you've invested in looking your best, the better you feel. This is certainly true for me anyway - getting my nails done, enhancing my naturally lacking lashes, having time to do my hair properly, having planned my outfit - all this adds to me enjoying the process and feeling fab and ready for fun when I step out the door. In contrast if I end up rushing to get ready with kids hanging off my ankles, no time for the pampering, and making a desperate grab for any old outfit, I'm feeling on the back foot and a bit stressed!

Getting press ready is much the same - the more you prepare behind closed doors the better you will feel when you head out into the world.

Let's address some questions we know others have had so you can move through these and enjoy the moment, if these are niggling you too.

CAN YOU GO OUT IF YOU'VE JUST TURNED 18?

Abso-bloody-lutely. Yes it's legal, so go for your life! The same goes for start-ups entering into the big wide world of PR! We often see female start-ups new to business hiding in corners rather than celebrating their big move, we see them get off to a very slow, conservative start because they don't really want to make any waves - they'd rather just do their thing in their little corner of the world and the fewer people who know about it the better. I was a bit like this when I first started out. I couldn't say I was a business owner - the words would not come out of my mouth. I felt like I was playing at it - even though I started my business working with multi-million pound clients. I didn't want to take the praise of people saying how brave or awesome I was as I didn't feel brave or awesome. I didn't take the credit for what I was bringing to the world because I spent my time underplaying it, so as not to sound like an egotistical so and so...! How crazy is this? What a time wasting process!

Don't let being a start-up stop you shouting about your business, or stop you capitalising on the power of PR! Start-ups are incredibly PR-able - you do not need twenty years experience to be PR ready - in fact a newly launching start-up is much easier to get in the press than a more established business. At start-up stage you're primed for press - please don't miss this opportunity, like I did.

HOW DO I DRESS TO IMPRESS?

How I dress has a huge impact on how I feel. When I 'dress for work' there is no doubt my activity is more supercharged than when I'm having a casual day in my trackies. There's something psychological about your outer appearance supporting your inner mood. It's the same with the media -how you present yourself to the media is EVERYTHING - and you need to be showing up as the best version of you as they won't stop to take a second look. Your clothing, your character, your brand photos, your credentials, your language, your passion and purpose, your qualifications, your back story, your mission statement, your authority goal, it all counts, and it all makes up the bigger image of how you're projecting yourself. How you put all this together speaks volumes.

Are you showing up as the creative playful soul you are? Are you exuding confidence through a bold choice of outfit choice? Do you make a statement with a bright lip and matching shoes...?

Think of your PR content as your party outfit - what presents you as the real you? What makes you attract attention, in the way you want, with the right vibe you want? Staying true to you and your character is absolutely key here as the success comes when you are not playing dress up in someone else's clothes, but you are so comfortable and confident in how you show up you exude confidence and credibility.

Tools to help you dress to impress for your PR party include:-

- Your Media Bio
- Your Brand Imagery
- Your Content Topics

Let's take these one at a time.

⚡ Your Media Bio

In our world your media bio is your PR bible - it's the one thing we insist all our clients have created before we start any press introductions, and it's something we've created and honed over the years to make our lives easier when pitching clients to journalists. Having come from a journalistic background really helps here as I know exactly the questions, they will ask of someone when trying to get to the bottom of their story. I know what they want to know, what they are interested in -and so we deliver this, from day one.

Our Media Bios have bagged our clients double page spread features - without ever having had to speak to a journalist - now I'm sure you'd like a bit of that?

Do you have a media bio? You might think that you do because many courses and coaches teach how to create a *one page bio* or even a *one para bio* - but that's not what we're talking about here, not for a long shot!

Our media bios are where you present yourself as the best version of you and you GIVE GIVE GIVE with your story, your mission, your passion, your purpose, your motivation, your struggles and triumphs. Due to the nature of the document, it ensures you've got clear on your mission message, your specialist areas of expertise, you've showcased your qualifications and experience and you've connected the dots of your own journey and backstory to your business. (NB this is a signature system at *Chocolate PR*).

This document can be anything from 3-6 pages of A4 long - it's a thorough look at who you really are and what you want to be known for - and to get to the end result it's such a powerful process.

You have to take time to reflect on things you may never have ever really thought about. You revisit old memories and join the dots about all the things that have made you, you. You bring through your highs, your lows, your struggles, your triumphs and through it all we see your values shine through and your character communicated. Soooo often revelations happen as part of the bio that are game changing in a much bigger way than just the PR side of things - revelations that change directions of businesses or dramatically challenge existing marketing content and tone as people realise they are not showing up as the real them, the them they want to be. And for new businesses it's total GOLD as they get to be PR-able from day one. They get to launch themselves into the world with carefully curated content that positions them at the top from day one. This stuff gives me goosebumps!

These are just some of the comments we regularly get about the media bios we create at Chocolate PR and the process....

"It made me cry" - This happens a lot! And it comes from a variety of different emotions. Often when we are at media bio stage the client is viewing their life journey as an outsider looking back in - they've been through the tough times and are out the other side and they are then looking back at the journey with fresh eyes. This can bring a myriad of emotions as people feel sad for 'the old' them, proud of 'the new' them

and empowered by their mission when they see it written down with real gusto on paper.

"I didn't recognise myself" many of our clients say. This comes down to Imposter Syndrome and them not previously having been able to see their value, to recognise the impact they are making or communicate their mission fiercely or powerfully enough. When we do this for them, and they read it back they are shocked by the mirror looking back at them. *"It made me proudly recognise all I have achieved"* we hear a lot. This is one of my favourite moments, when self-worth, and self-belief literally rises in front of my very eyes, This is a gift I love giving!

"It gave me the confidence to go all in with my business". Feeling like you ARE good enough, like you DO have a lot to offer the world and that you can clearly and confidently communicate it does wonders for your business. Suddenly you start to believe in yourself wholeheartedly, you get excited about what you're here to do, you recognise that you are different and that this is something to be embraced. Again, so magical, so special.

Perhaps I have digressed in terms of the role of the bio here - because fundamentally I planned to talk about it in the context of it being a tool to get you in the media - it kicks ass in doing that job but in reality I couldn't leave it at that because this is a PR tool that has so much more to give -it helps you feel good as well as look good and we all know how strongly the two are connected.

If you'd like to get an example media bio you can do so here

https://www.chocolatepr.co.uk/get-your-media-bio/

and get your hands on the questions we use to create it here -

https://www.chocolatepr.co.uk/whats-your-story-guide/

Your Brand Imagery

An important part of the media bio, and indeed any PR pitching is imagery as having a strong story only goes half the way to PR success. A national journalist we regularly work with, Lebby Eyres told us recently: *"If I don't have decent images I can't put the pitch forward to editors as they just won't consider it anymore without strong photos"*. In the old days you used to be able to get away with a cobbled together image but now the heat is on for the news sites and magazines to really attract the eyes of readers and keep them engaged so imagery has become more and more important. It's not just about that though, because not having decent PR photos is a missed opportunity. Remember the saying *'a picture tells a thousand words'* - well that's the job you want your imagery to do. You want your photos to reinforce your message, your character or elements of your story you want to showcase.

Think carefully about what you say in your pics - we need more than the standard headshot you use for LinkedIn, we need pictures with purpose, with passion. We often recommend using props, or your brand colours, or thinking about the location you have your pics taken in as these things all help.

If you're having a brand shoot and would love some inspiration we have a brand photography briefing sheet guide - just DM me on Insta if you'd like to get your hands on that (@jochocpr).

———

⚡ Your Content Topics

Being super clear on what subjects you are going to own is an important part of your PR prep. Stay super focused on what areas you will share your expertise on and don't deviate from these too much - because this is where you create traction. Over time you will become known as someone who is knowledgeable on these subject areas, you'll become an expert, you will become a go to spokesperson - but only if you have focus and don't spread yourself too thin. You will also become very searchable for such subjects online when you have PR stories on these subjects, and so will have created a digital footprint for your expertise - this way when journalists are searching for that subject area you are more likely to be found.

HOW MUCH IS TOO MUCH?

So you're getting prepared now, and are in full party mood. It's nice getting all glammed up and it's easy to get carried away with the excitement of it all isn't it? - the fake eyelashes come out, the hair extensions, the chicken fillets or Wonderbra maybe? (Haha back in the day!) And why not - do what makes you feel great!...but often we don't go the whole hog, rather we choose to draw it back in, for fear of what others might say or think.

We're all told that *'being too much'* is a bad thing in life - *'dull it down a bit' 'quieten down a bit' 'calm it down'* - Have you had any of these phrases thrown at you at any point? This is what happens in our day-to-day world as larger than life characters can be challenging to others - but this is NOT what we want for you in your PR. Do NOT dull yourself down, do not tone it down. Go all out in your fully marvellous glory.

Your job in PR is to stand out. To make PR work you have to dare to be different. You need to attract and hold the attention of journalists over and above the hundreds of other people they get approached by. You CANNOT be too much.

Remember the Queen Bee - *'I am Dani Wallace and I am the Queen Bee and I'm here to help you show up, wise up and rise up'* - YES Dani! This is exactly what we need - confidence, intrigue, purposeful showing up of a woman on a mission to make a difference in this world.

Have a think about how you could be a bit more standout? Could it be with your bio/title- how do you describe yourself? Is it doing you justice? We have rebranded clients to make them more PR-ale and it's a process I find really fun - we've changed L&D experts to *Team Happiness Strategists*, a declutterer to *THE realistic Home Organisation Expert* and we are also proud to represent *The Self Esteem Queen* and *The Branding Fairy Godmother* (both these names are their doing but we love bringing them to life)

Be brave and be bold in your representation of your skills and what you're an expert in - you gotta own it and having fun with it makes it feel lighter too.

FAKE I.D - CAN I FAKE IT 'TIL I MAKE IT?

Many of us may remember our forays into getting into night-clubs in our youth - fake I.Ds were very much a part of our world as we attempted to make it into clubs many years before our 18th birthdays! We'd recite our fake birthday a million times over so as not to be caught out by the tough looking bouncers whose job it was to interrogate us!

Faking it until you make it is something I have mixed feelings about in PR. I have to say I did love bouncing around clubs at fifteen years old, and so am grateful for what faking it brought me back then! - and to be honest I have been known to do a bit of *fake it 'til you make it* PR myself. It helps to present yourself as bigger than you are when you are going after big opportunities. If you're aiming high you need a rep that matches, and PR can defo help you with that.

PR can be a master of helping you *fake it 'til you make it* as it is very much a catalyst for creating a profile and image. YES - it can help create an image that makes you feel confident and purposeful, and it may create a perceived level of success that is greater than your current position and I don't think there is anything wrong with that - if you have got the experience and credibility behind you to make it happen. HOWEVER, I do not advocate fully faking it - being someone you're not. Use PR to amplify your brand, profile and message yes, but don't go making things up. Don't create a new persona for the purpose of your PR because this will come crashing down on you. So, even from the early days embrace who you really are and use your true values to drive your message.

HOW WILL I KNOW WHEN I'M READY?

If you go through the getting ready process and tick all the boxes, does this mean you are ready or will you still want a bit more time?

Do you remember the days back in your youth when you had hours to get ready? Not like these days when you're rushing out the door after having got the kids sorted and barely had time for a shower never mind all the fancy pampering we used to do? As a teen I remember never quite knowing when I was ready. One more change of outfit to decide? A bit more hairspray? Different earrings? A different bag? Change the shoes? There was always something to faff with, something to be indecisive about and usually this would make me late!

These days this 'faffing' is more likely to be something we do in our business, rather than in our personal lives and it may manifest as procrastination. I'm not ready to do PR – *'I'll just sort my website out'…' I don't have the right brand pictures'… 'I need to get my story straight'…* If those are your reasons just get on with it all - and get ready! However, if you're saying, *'I'm not ready because I'm too new in business'* or *'I'm not ready because I don't have enough clients or I'm not ready until I've done another course'* then this is all bull. These are faffing excuses like not being able to go out until you have a new dress - nonsense.

You don't want to be too late to the party that it starts without you, do you? You don't want to be stuck at home when everyone else is out having a ball because you didn't quite get ready in time? No, I didn't think so!

So - where do you sit, right now? Are you making faffing excuses, or do you have real work to do to prepare yourself for going out? Once you know you know and then you can move on! Be honest with yourself and give yourself a talking to if need be - because that PR party is waiting for you to be star of the show!

———

⚡ **Activity....**

(i) What barriers am I putting in my own way?

(ii) Which barriers are practical that need project planning and which are mindset related?

(iii) What actions do I need to take?

- This week
- This month

_____

_____

_____

_____

_____

_____

_____

_____

_____

_____

_____

_____

_____

_____

_____

Connect....

If you'd like a safe place to explore these thoughts, come and join us in our free group PR You Can Do It over on Facebook and you'll be surrounded by other like-minded women who've most certainly shared these same thoughts. We're all in it together. There is absolutely no need to do this alone xx

https://www.facebook.com/groups/PRYouCanDoIt

12

THE LIFE & SOUL OF THE PARTY - OR NOT

S o, we've talked about 'raising the roof' and we've talked about not following the path others do. You know I like you to dance to your own tune. But - what if you're not really a party person? What if you're not the one blasting out the karaoke, you'd much prefer to be snuggled under a blanket with your favourite box set... what then? Can you still host a good PR Party if you're not the life and soul of the party?

Yes, you blinkin' well can. I say this with total love and total compassion, because despite being able to step into being the life and soul of the party when needed there are definitely times when I'd prefer to be in my dressing gown with a hot chocolate in front of the fire!

You CAN still be a force to be reckoned with even if you're more nervous in the spotlight. You CAN very much be a leader in your space and still be challenged by Imposter

Syndrome. You can set the world alight with your message, even if all your brand elements aren't screaming 'I'm here'. But you CAN'T be the voice for your mission or message if you are hiding. You CAN'T represent the audience you are here to serve if you stay quiet. You CAN'T make a difference and make a change if you don't speak up.

But here's the thing - getting your PR foundations in place is the same no matter if you are super confident about being visible or less so. This stuff works whether you are an extrovert or an introvert, someone who embraces being seen or someone hugely nervous about putting themselves out there.

Most of our clients have Imposter Syndrome of some kind - just different types and levels, but the uniting factor that sees them all fight back against their own mindset challenges is their unwavering belief that their message matters more than their mind monkeys.

To really make an impact you must be brave. You must be bold. You must dare to be seen.

Yes, yes and yes, but moreover you must proudly stand behind your unique identity - and this is where the key lies. Your UNIQUE identity. Don't get wrapped up in trying to be someone else.

Don't play Agadoo remember. Do you.

This next client I am going to introduce you to, Hannah McKimm, has learnt to 'do her', after an inspired journey of self-development and support from the incredible Andrea

Callanan, the lady I often talk about having helped me tackle my Imposter Syndrome. Andrea saw in Hannah what I saw in Hannah - a woman so driven by her passion and purpose that it was essential she spoke out, a woman who was on an absolute mission to make a difference with her work, a woman who needed to make her story count.

Hannah joined us on our *Dare to Be Seen PR Accelerator* - an eight week support system for getting published in the press - after she'd completed her work with Andrea and was ready for her next steps and it was like this positive action taking was a signal to the world she was ready.

As we were working on creating Hannah's Media Bio (our PR goldmine of press ready media info) something significant happened. A story broke in the news that meant it was time for Hannah to step up. Feeling safe and supported by us, step up she did and *Oh My God* what impact this amazing lady made!

From having no understanding of PR to leveraging it in her business, Hannah learnt quick, and went from really struggling with the confidence of getting her story out there to sharing it on national TV! This example really shows you what's possible, no matter what stage you're at right now.

I'll let Hannah tell you more.

Hannah:

> *"I definitely had a passion and I knew there was a need for*

my work, but I didn't initially have the confidence to get it out there and that's why I joined Dare to Be Seen - to be in kind and caring hands where I could find my confidence - that was something Jo and the team gifted me."

"I am a therapist and coach, and I support ambitious women who are held back in their life and business by trauma. I help them break those chains of trauma to help them step into the life that they desire, but also I believe that they really deserve, because I know how it feels to feel trapped by trauma, to be defined by an experience, and I also know how it feels to break free from this haunting you. I specialise in helping women who have experienced sexual abuse, because that's my story."

This introduction in itself is a big deal. Initially Hannah didn't even mention the fact that she had a story connected to her specialism - she was presenting herself as a specialist therapist, but it wasn't clear, it was assumed, not offered as to why. This left question marks and the media don't like question marks - well none of us do really as we assume someone's hiding something, which they usually are.

As soon as Hannah was prepared to attach her story and use it to illustrate her mission magic happened. To hear her talk about her mission so clearly, and with such conviction is something that makes me massively, massively proud because I know the process it took to get there. When your story is one of trauma it isn't easy to relive it, but what we find in the PR process is actually that in getting your PR foundations in place, and building up your media bio, we go there and we deal with everything in one foul swoop, we make sense of it, we connect the dots, then we write it in a way that helps it make sense, that helps make it count in the work you are doing now, and things start to feel a bit easier.

If you're nervous about putting yourself out there getting to that point of really owning what it is you do and, and the importance of it and the impact of it is fuel for you. Hearing Hannah using words like *'breaking chains'*, makes me shout *'God Yes!'* because Jees that is what she is doing and to hear her really recognise that is so so powerful.

So why did Hannah decide PR was for her, despite feeling slightly terrified by the idea of it?

Hannah:

> *"I think for me, it just felt like the next natural progression from where I was. So, like I said, I was working with Andrea. I became a coach. I was starting to do other trainings, like brainspotting and adding to my skills but I, I wasn't getting out there. And then I heard people like Jo say - "People don't know this stuff about you until you share it with them and tell them" - and I just felt really compelled that I needed to share my message, but I didn't know how. I did know that Jo could help me though! The confidence that Jo had in the fact that she'd seen PR work for so many people before - people like me who were coaches and therapists and she'd seen the impact of that made me think yeah, this is this is where I need*

to go, because we can make a difference here and my story can change lives."

THIS is the secret here. When you can connect to the power of this, this is when you will find the faith, find the strength, find the confidence to get your message out. Hannah started to feel compelled to share her story and her knowledge after really connecting in her mind to the women who are still out there suffering as a result of traumatic experiences, not having found a way through it like she had. THIS pushed her to be brave and this became more real than she could have ever imagined when a story hit the news about the rise of drink spiking cases - the exact scenario which had led to Hannah's sexual abuse.

She knew this was her time to speak up and she bravely made it her moment to be a spokesperson for others, she committed to being a voice of hope and inspiration for others suffering.

Hannah:

"I think when I got to the stage of actually getting the story out there, it felt almost too easy in a way. Because I'd started to work on my message, on the importance of my story, on creating the media bio - I had got that message tuned and clear so that it was understandable for other people. We'd done that work - maybe not as much as we'd have liked as it was probably only a couple of weeks after I started on Dare To Be Seen that the story broke then I said "Right Jo, we've got to take this" but I still felt prepared".

To be ready to share a personal story like this you have to have done the internal work because there's a lot of emotion to process and we need to be sure how you'll respond in front of the media but we'd worked with Hannah and were convinced she was ready and she was clear and confident about how she was going to present herself.

What then happened was we effectively got to do live PR training, in real time as interview after interview came flooding in, after she made her first introduction to a local newspaper who were covering the story. Radio and TV followed, and we could take each opportunity and, using the bio as the basis think about what's the right part of the story to share in this instance or what advice do I need to be offering.

Hannah:

"At first I thought this was a really scary process as being live on TV was way out of my comfort zone but when I realised there were going to be no trick questions, when I realised I was there to provide hope and inspiration to others, not to re-live my trauma in mindless discussion the anxiety started to disperse and having my message so strongly crafted gave me the confidence to know that I had my foundations in place - I had a grounding to refer back to, whatever questions they asked and this made me feel a million times better. We got to evolve that message and hone it in real life circumstances"

And she was brilliant. She came across so naturally and had loads of compliments about her skills on camera because it looked second nature. When we know it wasn't second nature, that she still had huge fear then we see just how this is a massive, massive, big up that Hannah got herself to a point of looking so comfortable sharing a really, really emotional traumatic story for the good of the bigger picture.

Hannah:

> *"I was in the zone with that. I think it's because my why was more important than that fear, you know, I did all the right things leading up to it. I had my mindset in the right place. I did lots of grounding exercises. I talked to the right people, like Jo and Andrea. But really I had the confidence because I knew that what I had to say was important and it needed to be heard."*

Hannah could actually see the difference she could make by sharing her story - she knew there was something that she could actively do to make this situation better, or to stop other people from feeling so trapped by it and I think that's absolutely the answer. That is absolutely the thing to hold onto. Because when you are engulfed by that, it just starts to dumb down those fears and it puts them down the list in terms of importance, because you know this is something that you just HAVE to do - this is why you are here.

Hannah:

> *"For me, the more that I go out in the media and the more that I say what I need to say, and the more people get in touch to reach out and thank me and say it's given them so much*

hope the easier it all gets. As a result of my media work, I've been able to support incredible women who really needed me but hadn't previously been able to find me. I've had clients say 'I feel like I can let this go now', or 'I can see that I can heal from this because I can see that you've healed' - this is what I'm here for. Me speaking out has been a beacon to others who needed help. I became fully booked with clients following the PR. Getting out there and sharing my story has had an impact on so many levels. Also being quoted in national press as a 'the expert trauma coach' really reinforced to myself that I can step into that expert space and I do have the credibility to be trusted as a guide in this space by sharing my knowledge as well as my story."

This is something I love too that Hannah has been able to balance the PR from sharing her story and really connecting with people that way to now also sharing her knowledge, because she's been recognized as someone who is very very credible to speak in this space, so now she can educate through it as well, which is just brilliant. Now she's got her foot in the door she can elevate and amplify it.

Super, super exciting days.

Hannah:

"I've found the whole process extremely exhilarating and can't actually believe where I am now compared to how I felt when we first met. PR has been a vehicle that's enabled me to get my message and

mission out there, but also my passion and a huge part of the work I have done in prep for this has been really connecting to who I am and what I'm really here to do. It's now my intention to get out there in front of as many people as I can to show them who I am, as well as what I'm doing and why."

Well, that's music to my ears of course! This is EXACTLY why I do what I do - to get other women in business to believe that they can do it, even if they don't feel like they can at the beginning, even if they feel nervous and scared, like it's a massive, massive leap of faith, which it really is at the beginning -but they do it anyway.

Hannah, really stepped into this. She made herself proud. That, to me is being the life and soul of the party.

She used her expertise, her story, her opportunities - she didn't walk away despite her fears. She faced them head on - what a brilliant example of actually committing to using the power of PR. She's also now looking at her wider content and digging even deeper to see what else she can share to provide light-bulb moments to others.

Hannah:

"Everyone's got a story. I think mine is quite poignant and there was that defining moment for me, but also working with Chocolate PR helped me pull out those other bits and see there's other golden nuggets to my wider story that I wasn't really recognising, and I'm excited about exploring these further too now."

So, just look at that. From PR novice, to absolute PR Power-house, in a PR process that was a very short period of time. It did not take years to get to this point. There's no reason why you can't do this too.

If you're ready to say, *"I'm here to share this message"*, then things come to you and opportunities present themselves, and if you're ready to take those opportunities, then there's a whole new world out there for you. X

⚡ **Activity....**

Have you had any lightbulb moments reading this? Take a bit of time to reflect on your own circumstances and think about what parts of your story could empower and inspire others?

⚡ **HELP...**

For more info on Dare to Be Seen check out -

https://www.chocolatepr.co.uk/dare-to-be-seen/

Connect

Follow Hannah's journey at

https://www.instagram.com/hannahmckimmcoaching

https://www.facebook.com/hannahmckimmcoaching

13

OH WHAT A NIGHT!

 We are all of us stars and we deserve to twinkle"

— *MARILYN MONROE*

Y ou've done the work. You know the drill, now it's time to gooooooooooo to the party! Are you ready?

I want to ask you at this point if you've started to realise you're different? Are you ready to accept that you are meant to shine and twinkle?

As we've moved through the process of encouraging you to *Celebrate You* within this book have you started to honour the fact that you're special? Are you ready to own the fact that you're here because you have something unique to bring to the world? You have a talent, a gift, a story to share that will impact lives, and as a result this world will be a better place because you existed!

This can be stuff we shy away from, especially if affected by Imposter Syndrome - we feel uncomfortable taking on the power that we have, we feel egotistical for celebrating it. Well, I hope by now you're past all that? I hope by now you're feeling ready to step into the big shoes you have been given because entrepreneurs, especially passion and purpose fuelled ones, DO live in a parallel universe to *'ordinary people'* in many ways.

You are special. You are different to those who are stuck on the treadmill of their 9-5s, unhappy and lost as to what their options are, simply going through the motions and living an automated life. Maybe you've lived that life, but it's in the past.

 The greatest danger for most of us is not that our aim is too high and we miss it, but that it is too low and we reach it."

— MICHELANGELO

This is NOT you, and so you MUST make the most of your position. You MUST amplify your message to really make it count, to make the biggest difference you can with your work. This will make you feel different to those who are not in our world and this can feel odd at first. When you are being interviewed on TV or radio or your face is all over a women's magazine you are effectively given celebrity status - you are elevated -and rightly so. It's kinda like you're ushered off to the VIP part of the club, whilst others are left on the sticky dance floor - but don't feel bad about that! You don't belong on the sticky dance floor. You belong on the champagne swilling VIP table!

I believe it's a responsibility to own your mission and message and to step up and be a cheerleader and champion for it. I love this quote from Bono.

 We've got to follow through on our ideals or we betray something at the heart of who we really are"

Agreed?

Your day HAS come. You're the star of the party, your name is up in lights, you are being celebrated for your story, your journey, your knowledge and the contribution you are making to the world.

And you're ready, so let's drink it all in, one delicious sip at a time.

Remember that image you had when you imagined yourself being featured in your favourite magazine - well it's happened. The journalist trusted you as an expert because you proved to them that you had the knowledge, experience, and empathy to provide motivational content to their readers. They trusted you to be a guide because you shared your mission, your message, your passion, your story with them and now you get to inspire their readers and change lives with your knowledge sharing.

You offered up content that was perfect for their audience, and something timely that gave you a way in.

So, let's take a look at the winning formula?

What *is* your winning PR content that you see before you? What does it look like?

Is it your story you're sharing, or are you offering tips as well to highlight your point and showcase your expertise? Is it a pure thought leadership piece, a debate and discussion style piece? Or are you sharing a case study, a success story to show what's possible?

I want you to picture this so clearly you can see it printed in front of you. Here are some of the things you need to nail.

PICTURING YOUR PR

- What's your headline that draws your ideal clients in and engages them in an emotional interaction? Think about your tone and character (think back to the exercise of the chocolate bar and drink - what is your style) - will you shock or question, will you state facts or challenge facts, or will you encourage thoughts and evoke emotion? When you imagine your PR in print, what does it say? Remember short and snappy and to the point is the way to go here.
- What's the point you're going to be making in the piece? What are you using this PR piece for? What is the job it's doing? When you read it back why does it

make you feel accomplished? Because you're educated? Inspired? Challenged the status quo? What is the point of the article?

- What parts of your backstory are you going to share? Are you clear on what parts of your story you need to connect to your piece - what parts do you need to include to show empathy or understanding in relation to the subject matter? What does the reader need to know to help them trust in your knowledge or expertise?

- What knowledge are you going to impart? What are you going to teach them, what are the takeaways they can put into practice?

- What's the message you are leaving them with? How are you going to make them feel? Are you clear on the overall impact you want your article to have? Consider this at the start so you can be super clear when communicating this in your pitch

- How are you described? What's your title, what's your mini elevator pitch intro paragraph? Make sure you have both a one liner mini description of who you are and your job title as well as a one paragraph elevator pitch written in the third person – provide both so that the media can weave whichever works in.

[Check out our resources area to see some examples of these] **https://chocolatepr.co.uk/celebrating-you-with-pr/resources**

- What quote is the one that is going to be pulled out and highlighted within the piece - the really thought provoking one, the shocking one, the surprising fact, or the poignant part of your story? What will you be directing your readers attention to - consciously, confidently and creatively? When writing your article having things like this in mind make you more press ready and an asset to journalists which massively increases your chances of getting your stuff published.

- Lastly, consider what imagery is leaping off the page? Is it a highly slick brand photography shot that packs a punch or is it a more lifestyle relaxed shot of you that suits the tone of the piece more? What are you representing in this photo? What are you saying with this image?

Taking the time to answer these questions will ensure that you are showing up in the best way possible, in your full glory. We want you to shine at your PR Party, hell we want you to bloody well dazzle!

Imagine all that is done and it's bagged you an article in the very publication you've dreamt of. Now think again about how this feels? How does it really feel? From your toes to the top of your head and everywhere in between, when you see your name in print, your name quoted in the context of being an expert, your face showcased as a contributor to this publication?

Drink in this pride, this recognition, this validation, if you need it.

Now think again about how proud you are of having helped one more person, of having helped hundreds more people, of having helped thousands more people, as a result of your PR and bloody well celebrate this feeling!

When Niyc Pidgeon talks about the power of celebration from a positive psychology perspective she says...."Something truly magical happens when you frame your life with celebration...."

When our clients have shared with us their feelings after being celebrated in the press they say things like:-

"It feels surreal"

"It's like an out of body experience"

"I felt like I was looking at someone else"

"I am so energised!"

"I'm on a roll!"

"I'm ready to up level"

"I finally see that I AM an expert"

"I now appreciate the power of my story"

Celebrate it all.

You should be super proud of being prepared to be vulnerable. You should be super proud of having faced your fears. You should be super proud of being a part of the ripple effect. This is part of your legacy. Your story has the power to change the direction of someone else's story. And this needs to be honoured.

Have the drinks, eat the cake, dance like a crazy person. You deserve it all. You've earnt this party and the opportunity to celebrate you! You've experienced the blood, sweat and tears for it, you've dug deep for it - which makes it all the sweeter. You're making your story count.

The feeling we get at team Choc PR when we secure our clients incredible coverage NEVER gets old. We are in party mood EVERY single time. Imagine how you will feel owning this feeling yourself, knowing you've done all the hard work to get there - bloody amazing!

So, let's do it.

Action time.

Make the pitch!

Once you've got clear on all of the above, here are a few top tips on how to actually introduce yourself to your target journalists.

HOW TO PITCH

This advice is based on you making a proactive pitch - i.e. you are taking an idea to a journalist 'cold' rather than pitching them something on the back of a journo request call out. This is 'old school' PR but defo still very much a skill in demand if you want to take control of your PR activity and not just be at the beck and call of what the journalists want to write about.

You want to set your own agenda?

Follow this process and let's get your article ideas out there!

(i) **Pre-work**. Before we dive into the pitch email don't forget PR is all about connection, so in advance make sure you have identified key journalists you are going to pitch to, and you've been interacting with them on Twitter, or Instagram. Make sure you have their contact details ready.

(ii) **The intro email.** These days phone pitches have become less of a thing, so email pitches are the thing to master. You want this email to be short and direct but provide enough info for them to make a judgment that what you're offering is of great value to their readers. Make this friendly - no Dear Sirs etc here - you want to connect on a human-to-human level. Add a bit of chit chat in- a sentence will do, but something to soften the intro rather than it being immediately - *please publish me.* If you've picked something up from their socials, or seen a recent article they've written it's nice to mention that. Make this email as personal as possible.

Once that's out of the way then get straight to the point. Tell them that after researching the types of articles they write you can see a synergy between their subject areas and your own and you'd like to propose an article for the xxx section of their publication or the xxxx feature they write. (The more specific you can be the better -i.e. the Family section, the Health section, the tips section, The Inspiring Women profiles etc.)

Then tell them:-

- Who you are (with your para intro of *'I am, and I, so that, because"*
- The Headline idea
- The article overview (key points you'll cover, key messages and end goal)
- The takeaways and any free resources you can also offer
- Give a nod to your story and why you care about this subject, letting them know what you're prepared to share if it's tips you are pitching. If it's a Real-Life Story you are going for then the story is the focus
- Attach a couple of low res images or links to images so they can see you are press ready and get a feel for how this would look on a page.

There you go, as easy as that. You've opened the door, you've started the conversation, you've invited them to your PR Party.....whoop whoop! - but we don't stop there.

(iii) **Follow up**. As we know this may not lead to a direct hit, much as we'd love to see your face in the paper the next day from just sending this email, so make sure you also schedule in some follow up. This is kinda like when you've invited someone to your party and you're waiting for their RSVP -you might give them a little nudge to confirm they are coming.

Sometimes that's what journalists need - a little nudge - just a gentle nudge, a polite one, not a great big shove, to remind them of your email and pitch. Their lives are busy, their inboxes more so, so be prepared to follow up to get back to the top of the pile again. In this follow up we don't want to say *'are you going to publish my piece'* - much as you'll be dying to ask this, it is the sure fire way to piss them off. Approach this is from a place of being helpful or topical.

You say things like:-

- 'I just thought I'd check in after sending you my article idea last week after seeing yet more discussion around xxx in the national news -I'd love to bring my perspective on this to your readers to help balance out this debate'
- After sending you my pitch idea I have had a further thought about how this could work…
- I just wanted to check you'd seen my pitch idea as it was timely to xxxxx (if attached to an awareness day or diary date)

You need to be seen as being helpful not harassing. Useful not annoying. Supportive, not pushy. Keep this in mind with your tone and sense check that whilst you are desperate for them to just tell you that they are going to use your article you cannot come across as a needy Nelly! - No-one wants to go to *their* party!

Keep in touch, but not too much and if it goes dead on you, then it's time to look for a new idea. Don't be scared to keep pitching but make sure what you are pitching is as targeted as possible and you're coming at it from the angle of what they need, not just what you want to say.

MAKE THE MOVE

Activity… & HELP…

Get clear on all this then DM me who you want to approach. I'm here to help you make this happen. DM me @jochocpr via Insta and ask me specifically for the journalist's contact details you want. Do your research first to make sure you're inviting the right person to the party, find out who writes about your subject area, where there's a good fit, then let's do this. I can't wait to be celebrating with you!

And remember - this is all a game. PR is a game that shouldn't be taken too seriously, even if your subject matter is deep. That's not said to belittle your content or the power of what you have to share, but to stop this feeling heavy and to take the pressure off a bit.

Let's do this together and enjoy the process, let's be playful, let's be creative, and let's have some fun along the way.

> *People rarely succeed unless they have fun in what they are doing."*
>
> — DALE CARNEGIE

Enjoy and embrace the experience and you will reap the rewards.

14

UNLEASHED AND UNAPOLOGETIC!

I t's your time! It's your moment.
Shout it out LOUD!

Give me a C: "C"

Give me an E: "E"

Give me an L: "L"

Give me an E: "E"

Give me a B: "B"

Give me a R: "R"

Give me an A: "A"

Give me a T: "T"

Give me a E:"E"

Yes!

You've done it! It's now time to enjoy the ride. As we wrap up what has been quite a journey together I want to arm you with some ammo around what next, because blimey it doesn't stop here, oh no, the celebrations continue!

You've been to the party - but now it's afterparty time….oh yes - we never let up!!

In this final chapter we're going to be looking at what to do with your PR, how to use it to grow your business and to open doors to new opportunities.

What's coming next? Oh, you've been shortlisted for a national award? Congratulations! Oh, you've been offered a paid speaking gig? Awesome! Oh, what's that, a well-known brand has approached you about a collaboration to their one million followers? Cool.

"And so it is……."

This is something my good friends and Mastermind sisters, Donna & Cheryl from *Now is Your Time* say a lot and it's something I want you to embrace.

We can only capitalise on the opportunities that are out there for us if we dare to see them, and once we've seen them, we need to embrace them, feel them and love on them, to bring them into our futures…*and so it is.*

What would you like to come from your PR activity? If you dreamt with no limits, where would it take you?

Make a note of your aspirations, commit them to writing, and let them be your next adventure.

I hope you're thinking big and please do share with me on Instagram @jochocpr what your goals are - you never know, I may be able to help you make them happen!

To get you off the ground I'll share some easy, natural first steps you can take once you've bagged your PR coverage, to make sure it's working hard for you.

The power of your PR doesn't just lie in the coverage itself, it lies in what you do with it, because the joy of celebrating you is a gift that keeps on giving.

Your audience loves to have something to get excited about and PR is one of those things that really does create a buzz. You get PR and people think you're famous. You get PR, people elevate you to expert status. You get PR and others have NO clue how you've done it and are SUPER impressed - this often creates epic engagement on social and a ripple effect that just keeps giving.

You must milk this!

HOW TO CAPITALISE ON YOUR PR

When you get PR make sure you:-

Post the hell out of it.

Post it when it happens - celebrating it, sharing your genuine reaction about being published and what this means to you. Don't play it down and try to be super cool about it as part of the magic of sharing things with your audience is sharing how much spreading your message means to you.

Tag the publication and thank them for helping to share your message/create conversation around the subject etc. Remember when sharing it if the article is in print don't post a picture of the whole thing as you are asking for trouble - you are not allowed to share print content without a license - so either take a video of you perusing the piece, or share an image of a section of the piece. If it's online then of course share the link so people can read the whole article there - that's totally fine and encouraged.

After your initial post share it again a few days later, sharing the response you've had to it and you're so pleased you decided to put your story/advice out there because you can already see the impact it's making. This gets the piece in front of anyone who missed it and back in front of those who did see it and for them you're further building your credibility.

Then once the week is done, remember not to bury this. Schedule and repurpose the piece for future posts - maybe attach to something timely or topical in future or just use it as a throwback post or a reminder about the subject matter. Rinse and repeat. Rinse and repeat. Make this work hard for you, don't let it be a one hit wonder.

MAKE IT A PART OF YOUR FURNITURE.

This is where the fabulous term *Trust Tags* comes in. When you've been featured in the media you can say *'As Seen in'* or *'As Featured in'* and add the logos of the publications you have featured in to all your marketing. It's psychologically proven to increase the trust factor with potential customers when you have media logos on your banner on your sales page - you get fast tracked credibility from their third party endorsement. When you've earnt these *Trust Tags* make sure they are working for you. Get them on your sales pages, on your homepage, on your social media headers, on your email signatures, on your business cards. Anywhere a new contact could come into contact with you - hit them with it.

Below is an example of what they can look like when turned into an image to be used as a banner... pretty damn cool right?!

AS SEEN IN...

PROACTIVELY USE IT TO START NEW CONVERSATIONS

1. **On social media**. For everyone who comments on your post when you share your PR this is a door opener opportunity to follow up the conversation with them, whether on the post itself or in the DMs. By commenting on your post, they have come out of the woodwork to congratulate you and to show they are impressed with you, so take that and run with it. Use it as a chance to strike up conversation and get interaction going - you never know where this could lead.

2. **In DMS**. If you have warm leads who you could do with following up, using press coverage is a nice way to progress the convo - sharing your article because you think they might be interested in the content is a

great way to show support and also elevate you at the
same time.

3. **With potential partners.** When we work with clients
   in our *Make Me Famous Mastermind* or 121 we often
   explore the power of collaborations and consider who
   we could approach for wider PR campaign activity.
   Having PR under your belt makes this introduction so
   much more powerful as it shows you are already a
   thought leader in your space, and you are actively
   bringing something to the party and contributing to a
   wider mission. You could send this via a LinkedIn
   message or tag them on social then DM them to say
   why you think together you could take this
   conversation further.... We've seen really exciting
   collabs happen as a result of this approach which has
   got our clients in front of huge new audiences of ideal
   clients.

4. **To get podcast guests.** If you're looking for podcast
   guests who already have a profile then introducing
   yourself via your PR is a great way to get yourself on a
   level with them (whether or not you are anywhere
   near their level or not!) It's also a great way to show
   you are walking the walk of representing your core
   subject area and of giving them a flavour of your tone
   and approach. You could invite them to discuss
   elements from the piece, or their experiences around
   said subject.

5. **Use it to get speaking gigs - online and IRL.** Much
   like when approaching podcast guests, when
   introducing yourself to event organisers or online

community managers via PR you have a powerful first interaction. These people are usually looking for experts and storytellers - people on a mission to use their skills and experience to improve the lives of others and they are looking for people who are credible. They don't want to take a punt on any Tom, Dick or Harry who says they are on a mission to change the world but is offering no evidence of any such thing. Likewise, they need someone who is trusted to deliver via their expertise, not someone who just likes the sound of their own voice. PR helps showcase you at the right level from your first approach and it can fast track the process of you being picked.

6. **Use it to enter awards**. Winning awards is a funny old game. We've seen clients enter the same awards year on year and not win anything, despite doing incredible work, but then do some PR and gain some awesome trust tags and reach and re-enter to win. Again, this comes down to perception - the judges trust you more -but it also comes down to being able to prove you're walking your walk. When you've got PR under your belt you can confidently say you are spreading your message to millions, you can show what discussions you are starting, what knowledge you are sharing, what impact you are making and that goes down a treat when ticking boxes on awards entries. You go further than those who are just talking the talk, you are very clearly walking the walk

7. **Use it to fuel more PR.** Once you have your first piece of PR I guarantee it'll leave you hungry for more - it's quite addictive and it's also quite natural that PR fuels PR - so it creates its own ripple effect often without you doing anything further. On many occasions we've seen clients be approached by national media after featuring in their local press and often this comes inbound, but if not take it to them. Up-level local to national by sharing your local news story with a national journo to show the story has been picked up, but say you'd love to share it on a bigger scale. Freelance journalists are often good at taking on these missions so that's something to think about - sending your article to them and asking them where else they think they could pitch it

8. **Use it to sell.** On the back of generating national PR we have had clients bag 50K contracts through sharing their article on *LinkedIn*, become fully booked in a matter of weeks after sharing their story that really spoke to their niche audience, and create new programmes with a wait list because of the buzz they generated. This happens and often it comes naturally but you can also be proactive. Use your PR in your email marketing, use it in your comms with prospects, USE it everywhere! Remember PR fast tracks the know like and trust factor, so use it so it can do its job!

These are all ways you can make your PR efforts really count in your business because I'm all for doing things with purpose. I fully appreciate the emotional effort and the time commitment that goes into getting yourself PR ready and I want you to be able to maximize the impact.

PR has been game changing for so many of our incredible clients:-

This is what it means to some of the clients I have introduced you to:-

Louisa Herridge:

I think PR means to me visibility, credibility, and cele-brating success, because I've been able to do all of those through the media and beyond. Through PR I've really defined how I show up, I've been brave and bold and my audience has loved that, they love the vulnerability I'm prepared to show so they know I understand what they're going through and they've taken the PR as a sign of me being credible, from so early on in my busi-ness. This has 100% fast tracked my growth. I can't think of any other medium that would have enabled all that in such a short space of time. Through having such a strong profile I've been able to attract dream clients - clients who need me, clients whose lives I have changed as a result of my work and that's pretty amazing!"

Hannah McKimm:

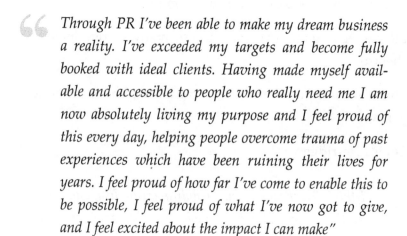

Through PR I've been able to make my dream business a reality. I've exceeded my targets and become fully booked with ideal clients. Having made myself available and accessible to people who really need me I am now absolutely living my purpose and I feel proud of this every day, helping people overcome trauma of past experiences which have been ruining their lives for years. I feel proud of how far I've come to enable this to be possible, I feel proud of what I've now got to give, and I feel excited about the impact I can make"

Dani Wallace:

I'm not one for doing things by halves - I go all in - and then some! - and this is how I launched my business - I decided from very early on that PR would play a key role in me being seen and spreading my message and it has. I entered the marketplace as if I'd been there years and this was very intentional. I got my story straight early on, I made it make sense and used my Media Bio as a way to communicate what I stand for. Over the past three years I've consistently been in national newspapers, magazines, on TV and radio debates and on BBC news sharing my story, expertise and mission. As well as helping me grow my business this has won me awards and connected me to celebs, influencers and global entrepreneurs who I've then gone on to work with to create a ripple effect together. PR has helped me to help others - it's given me a platform to be that hand that reaches back for those who are where I was and for them to see a beacon of hope and I'm super grateful for this."

THIS is why I am on a mission.

THIS is why I do what I do.

Because the work we do empowers. The work we do ignites. The work we do changes lives.

There I've said it. The work we do changes lives.

Others have said it many many times, but I've shied away from it and brushed these comments under the carpet, overwhelmed by the gravitas of such a statement. But as part of my experience writing this book I've stepped even more deeply into my own sense of purpose, as well as getting excited about yours, and I feel ALL the feels for the impact we can make together. When I can help you speak out and share your story and knowledge and expertise, you can help others see what's possible. When I help you celebrate you and your journey you can help others see that they could one day celebrate turning a corner in their life too. The energy of celebration is infectious. The energy of celebration should be celebrated!

So, welcome to the party, welcome to your celebration, welcome to the journey of *Celebrating YOU!*

I've loved getting ready with you, of preparing you for the limelight, now pass the bubbles, and let's toast - To *Celebrating* **YOU.**

P.S There's a party playlist waiting to spur you on at:

https://chocolatepr.co.uk/celebrating-you-with-pr/resources.

Let's have some fun! X

P.P.S Your life is your story, make it count xx

WHAT NEXT? IT'S AFTER PARTY TIME!

HOW CAN I SUPPORT YOU FURTHER?

Hello again! I love that you're on this page! Whether you've taken in all the info from each and every chapter and you're ready for more or you've skipped to this page without reading the entire book I love you either way- because you're open to me being a part of your onward PR journey!

PR is a specialist area. Whilst my mission with this book has been to get you to a point of seeing how you can use PR to celebrate you, your business and your story and to get you feeling more confident about getting yourself out there via the media, by sharing with you how to play the game, I fully appreciate that there may have been parts that went over your head, or times when you wanted to recoil and say *'I can't do this'*. You CAN do this, but sometimes you need a helping hand to get you there. If you do, I'm here, and so is my team, to support and guide you further.

If you need more hand holding, we've got you.

If you want more personal direction, we've got you.

If you're feeling supercharged and ready to smash it, we've got you.

If you have absolutely no intention of undertaking any of this PR shiz yourself and just want it taken off your hands, we've got you.

I say we, because I can offer you more than just me in the form of cheerleaders and champions. I have an incredible team who work with me at Chocolate PR and one particular special lady needs a mention here. I did already shout her out in the dedications as

she has played a huge part in my mission over the last few years but here I want to tell you a little more about her.

'Jo M' is one of the key people you get to work with when you work with us at Chocolate PR. She has her ear to the ground and her eyes on the news, always looking for the door opener opportunities for you. She is a comms goddess with twenty years' experience but more than that she has the biggest heart and when you come into the fold she joins me in embracing you! A coach as well as a PR she also brings huge empathy to the table in terms of understanding how you feel throughout the daring to be seen process and as an Imposter Syndrome sufferer herself she gets it when you say *'I'm not good enough'* -

but she won't let you believe it for long. I am so proud of what we achieve together and I'd love for us to support you further.

HERE'S HOW YOU CAN WORK WITH ME AND MY TEAM AT CHOCOLATE PR

1) **Done For You PR** - We take it all off your hands and manage media liaison for you. Usually comes with a press release or media bio for *Proactive PR* or we can be your eyes and ears for inbound journo request opportunities

(Media Bios can also be stand-alone projects)

2. **PR Coaching & Mentoring** - We work with you over a 30 or 60 day or agreed period to coach you into the press. Weekly 121 calls, media contacts, content editing and pitching support

3. **PR Courses** - Learn how to get your story straight with our four-week entry level digital course StorySteps (with live Q&A support) or prepare to get published in the media in eight weeks via *Dare To Be Seen* - our much loved PR Accelerator which walks you through how PR works and what you need to do to get in the press. We handhold you and help you edit your content to get your PR ready as well as working to support you with any limiting beliefs or Imposter Syndrome that may be blocking you along the way

4. **Get in The Press- Live!** - Our low-cost membership giving you access to live PR opportunities and guidance to help you fast track your national media trust tags. With live Q&As and coaching support you can tap into the team and be inspired by the community - win win. Month by month, no tie ins.

5. **Make Me Famous Mastermind** - A supercharged space for when you really want to nail your place as an expert in your field, we look at awards, PR campaigns and collaborations as well as all things media. This is for people who KNOW they want to be recognised for what they do so they can make more impact on a bigger scale. Six-month container, small group with some 121 support. ✻

6. **VIP PR Party** - An exciting 121 intensive experience where we get creative and strategic and we map out your PR plan for the next six months in fun inspiring settings. We get your story straight, your PR angles nailed and identify your press opportunities over the next 6 months. You also pitch live to a journalist, and we have fun with media training (in person) as well as introducing you to a wider hit list of media with me right by your side. This will supercharge your PR journey and get you set for success 🔥

For full info see www.chocolatepr.co.uk

*If you get in touch to enquire tell me you're a reader of 'Celebrating You' and if we work together there will be an extra little treat in store for you too *

P.S Don't Forget you can also hang out with us for free at **https://www.facebook.com/groups/PRYouCanDoIt** and you can get more of my words of encouragement via my Podcast PR Powerhouse - find it on your preferred podcast app here - **https://podfollow.com/pr-powerhouse**

We've come this far! Don't be a stranger!! xx

Lightning Source UK Ltd.
Milton Keynes UK
UKHW021851120922
408771UK00009B/175/J